Philippians

Live as a citizen worthy of the gospel of Christ

ISBN No: 1-905975-02-3

Published by Biblical Frameworks Limited

Reg. Office: St Paul's Church, Robert Adam Street, London W10 3HW

Cover design, typesetting and production management by Verité CM Ltd, Worthing, West Sussex UK +44 (0) 1903 241975

Illustrations by Richard Thomas

Printed in England

Biblical Frameworks is registered in England No: 5712581

Contents

Bookby**Book**

Bible Study hints and helps

'Citizens of heaven'

Philippians

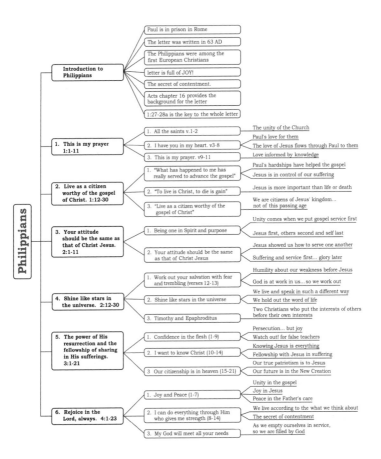

Philippians

Introduction to Philippians
- Paul is in prison in Rome
- The letter was written in 63 AD
- The Philippians were among the first European Christians
- letter is full of JOY!
- The secret of contentment.
- Acts chapter 16 provides the background for the letter
- 1:27-28a is the key to the whole letter

1. This is my prayer 1:1-11
- 1. All the saints v.1-2
  - The unity of the Church
  - Paul's love for them
- 2. I have you in my heart. v3-8
  - The love of Jesus flows through Paul to them
- 3. This is my prayer. v9-11
  - Love informed by knowledge

2. Live as a citizen worthy of the gospel of Christ. 1:12-30
- 1. "What has happened to me has really served to advance the gospel"
  - Paul's hardships have helped the gospel
  - Jesus is in control of our suffering
- 2. "To live is Christ, to die is gain"
  - Jesus is more important than life or death
- 3. "Live as a citizen worthy of the gospel of Christ"
  - We are citizens of Jesus' kingdom... not of this passing age

3. Your attitude should be the same as that of Christ Jesus. 2:1-11
- 1. Being one in Spirit and purpose
  - Unity comes when we put gospel service first
  - Jesus first, others second and self last
- 2. Your attitude should be the same as that of Christ Jesus
  - Jesus showed us how to serve one another
  - Suffering and service first... glory later

4. Shine like stars in the universe. 2:12-30
- 1. Work out your salvation with fear and trembling (verses 12-13)
  - Humility about our weakness before Jesus
  - God is at work in us... so we work out
- 2. Shine like stars in the universe
  - We live and speak in such a different way
  - We hold out the word of life
- 3. Timothy and Epaphroditus
  - Two Christians who put the interests of others before their own interests

5. The power of His resurrection and the fellowship of sharing in His sufferings. 3:1-21
- 1. Confidence in the flesh (1-9)
  - Persecution... but joy
  - Watch out! for false teachers
  - Knowing Jesus is everything
- 2. I want to know Christ (10-14)
  - Fellowship with Jesus in suffering
- 3 Our citizenship is in heaven (15-21)
  - Our true patriotism is to Jesus
  - Our future is in the New Creation

6. Rejoice in the Lord, always. 4:1-23
- 1. Joy and Peace (1-7)
  - Unity in the gospel
  - Joy in Jesus
  - Peace in the Father's care
- 2. I can do everything through Him who gives me strength (8-14)
  - We live according to the what we think about
  - The secret of contentment
- 3. My God will meet all your needs
  - As we empty ourselves in service, so we are filled by God

Introduction

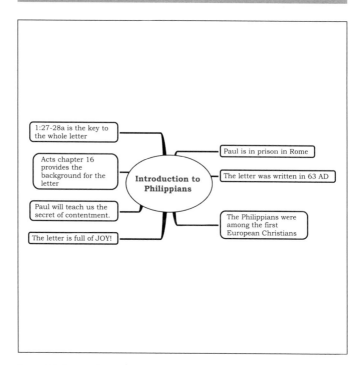

Be Joyful! "Joy is the music that runs through this epistle, the sunshine that spreads over all of it. The whole epistle radiates joy and happiness." [1]

The letter of Philippians was written by Paul while he was in prison in Rome in about 63AD, but there is no bitterness or disillusionment here. In this letter Paul opens his heart to us, showing us the secret to real joy in every circumstance. The letter speaks of fellowship in the sufferings of Jesus, and yet there is no book of the Bible so full of joy.

---

[1] Lenski, *The Interpretation of St Paul's epistles to the Galatians, to the Ephesians and to the Philippians*, Hendrikson, 1988, page 691

In this book the apostle Paul will share with us the secret of contentment. He will show us how to know true contentment at all times, no matter what hardships we have to face. He will show us that real joy does not depend on circumstances, but should be the constant possession of every citizen of heaven.

Within probably 50 years of Paul's letter, a great Christian leader called Polycarp wrote a letter to the Philippians where he speaks very highly of Paul's letter:

> "These things, brethren, I write to you concerning righteousness, not because I take anything upon myself, but because you have invited me to do so. For neither I, nor any other such one, can come up to the wisdom of the blessed and glorified Paul. He, when among you, accurately and steadfastly taught the word of truth in the presence of those who were then alive. And when absent from you, he wrote you a letter, which, if you carefully study, you will find to be the means of building you up in that faith which has been given you, and which, being followed by hope, and preceded by love towards God, and Christ, and our neighbour, 'is the mother of us all.' "[2]

Polycarp knew that he could never write with the divinely inspired wisdom of the great apostle Paul, so he was happy to point the Philippians to Paul's letter so that they could grow to spiritual maturity.

Why did Paul write the letter? Paul planted the church in Philippi, as we read in Acts 16, but his arrival in Philippi is packed with divine providence. At the beginning of Acts 16 Paul brought Timothy along with him.[3] In verse 6 the Holy Spirit prevented Paul from going into the province of Asia. Then, Acts 16:7-8 "When they came to the border of Mysia, they tried to enter Bithynia, but the Spirit of Jesus would not allow them to. So they passed by Mysia and went down to Troas."

It seemed that every direction they took was blocked by the Holy Spirit. However, a momentous event happened to the apostle Paul; an event that would change the direction of European history.

---

[2] Chapter 3 of Polycarp's Epistle to the Philippians. We have included the complete text of Polycarp's letter on our website: www.biblicalframeworks.com

[3] Notice from verse 10 how Luke is also in the party, because he writes using 'we' and 'us'.

Acts 16:9-12 "Paul had a vision of a man of Macedonia standing and begging him, 'Come over to Macedonia and help us.' After Paul had seen the vision, we got ready at once to leave for Macedonia, concluding that God had called us to preach the gospel to them. From Troas we put out to sea and sailed straight for Samothrace, and the next day on to Neapolis. From there we travelled to *Philippi,* a Roman colony and the leading city of that district of Macedonia."

The Holy Spirit was determined to get Paul into Europe, and his first European mission was in *Philippi.*

After Lydia believed the gospel, Paul's mission team had a place to stay. The spiritual world knew the significance of the arrival of the apostolic mission team, and one spirit through a young girl declared, "These men are servants of the Most High God, who are telling you the way to be saved" (verse 17). When Paul drove that spirit out of the girl, in the Name of Jesus, he was involved in a clash with the civic authorities.

Luke is very careful to explain the issues of civic authority and law in Philippi because they were critical to life in that city. The crowd (verses 20-21) "brought them before the magistrates and said, 'These men are Jews, and are throwing our city into an uproar by advocating customs unlawful for us Romans to accept or practise.'" Notice how the crowd are so anxious to be the very best Roman citizens. We sense the pride these people felt about having the privileges of Roman law and citizenship. With this in mind, we can understand more of what is going on at the conclusion of Acts 16.

Acts 16:37-40 "Paul said to the officers: 'They beat us publicly without a trial, even though we are Roman citizens, and threw us into prison. And now do they want to get rid of us quietly? No! Let them come themselves and escort us out.' The officers reported this to the magistrates, and when they heard that Paul and Silas were Roman citizens, they were alarmed. They came to appease them and escorted them from the prison, requesting them to leave the city. After Paul and Silas came out of the prison, they went to Lydia's house, where they met with the brothers and encouraged them. Then they left."

The Philippians took Roman citizenship very seriously and were deeply shaken when they saw how they had illegally treated Roman citizens. What would Rome think of this kind of behaviour?

Paul knew that the Church must not be classified as a politically dangerous organisation. It was vital that the Roman Empire realise that the followers of Jesus were the very best citizens. That is why Paul made sure that the magistrates give a public vindication of himself and Silas.

So, the Philippians highly valued *Roman* citizenship and we will see that theme in Paul's letter.

A key theme of the book is the unity of the church in the gospel. How important this message is today! On the one hand, there are those who speak a great deal about church unity, but don't explain what it is that truly unites us in truth and purpose. Truth always runs a very poor second to unity in such thinking. What are we united about if we are not clear on the gospel itself? On the other hand, there are those who love truth much more than unity. For them, specific systems of doctrine will always win over Christian fellowship. They will all too easily divide from gospel-loving fellow Christians. Paul teaches us how to grasp truth and unity in a proper balance.

The letter of Philippians teaches us important lessons. In many ways 1:27-28a is a summary of the whole letter. We have seen that 'being a citizen' was at the heart of life in Philippi, so Paul speaks of being a citizen in 1:27. However, this is not clear in many English translations, so we have corrected the NIV translation below.

> **1:27-28a** "Whatever happens, *live as a citizen worthy of the gospel of Christ*. Then, whether I come and see you or only hear about you in my absence, I will know that you stand firm in one spirit, contending as one man for the faith of the gospel without being frightened in any way by those who oppose you."

Notice the balance of truth and unity. The faith of the gospel is the banner under which the church gathers, when we gather together, united against our real opponents. That is how we are true citizens of Christ's kingdom, which is so much more than all the kingdoms of this passing age.

We know true contentment as we give ourselves away for others in the service of Jesus. You can never grasp fulfilment if you are pursuing it for yourself. It is only when we forget ourselves and live for Jesus that we discover true contentment and joy.

AD	THE LIFE OF THE APOSTLE PAUL
10?	Born and educated at Tarsus.
37-40	Paul's meeting with Jesus on the road to Damascus, followed by three years personal training from Jesus in the desert. Galatians 1:17.
45-48	*Paul's first missionary journey.* Antioch, Seleucia, Salamis, Paphos, Perga, Pisidian Antioch, Iconium, Lystra, Derbe, and Attalia. Acts 13:13-14:28
49	Council of Jerusalem – Acts 15.
50-52	**1 & 2 Thessalonians**
50-53	*Paul's second missionary journey.* Jerusalem, Antioch, Derbe, Lystra, Troas, Neapolis, Philippi, Amphipolis, Apollonia, Thessalonica, Berea, Athens, Corinth, Cenchreae, Ephesus, and Caesarea. Acts 15-18:22.
55-57	**Galatians**
54-58	*Paul's third missionary journey.* Antioch, Ephesus, Thessalonica, Corinth, Philippi, Troas, Assos, Mitylene, Miletus, Tyre, Caesarea, and Jerusalem. Acts 18-21.
57	**1 & 2 Corinthians, within a year of each other.**
57-58	**Romans**
58-60	Paul in prison in Judea
60-61	Journey to Rome
61-63	In prison in Rome
62-63	**Ephesians, Philippians, Colossians, Philemon**
63-67	Other journeys. He may well have made it to Spain, as he wanted – Romans 1:10, 15:24, 28; 16:1-5. In Clement's first letter to the Corinthians he seems to indicate that Paul accomplished this desire. "After preaching both in the east and west, he gained the illustrious reputation due to his faith, having taught righteousness to the whole world, and come to the extreme limit of the west, and suffered martyrdom under the prefects". *He presumably also visited the Philippians again, as he seems to assume he will be able to do in 1:25-26.*
64-65	**Titus; 1 Timothy; (Hebrews – Paul is a possible writer)**
66-67	**2 Timothy**

1. This is my prayer. 1:1-11

'Fellowship in sufferings'

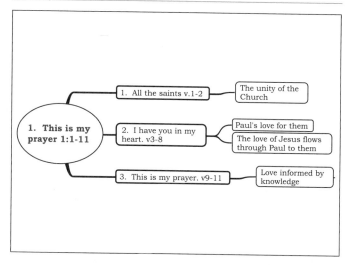

1. TO ALL THE SAINTS (1-2)

The great theme of the Philippian letter is the united fellowship of the Church. We find our joy and fulfilment when we focus on serving the needs of others rather than on our own perceived needs. The Christian family must have a higher priority than our own individual lives.

In the modern world there is so much pressure to focus on our own individual lives and families, to be self-centred. This wonderful part of God's Word shows us how to escape the prison of self-interest into the freedom of Jesus. Putting the needs of others before our own needs may seem unattractive to us, yet this self-sacrifice will set us free and unite us together in Jesus. There is nothing so vital to the health and purpose of the Church of Jesus Christ as her unity in the gospel. We will see that theme in the letter time after time.

We will see how the unity that comes from faithful gospel work is the only way that a local church can experience genuine Christian unity and fellowship. Paul will set evangelism as the rallying point where any church can find genuine, deep unity, no matter how diverse they may be.

As a kind of preview of this we see that the letter is written by both Paul and Timothy, and it is addressed to "all the saints... together with the overseers and deacons" (verse 1). Paul and Timothy are united in their letter writing and the whole church at Phillipi is included in the address.

However, the sense of unity goes even further in verse 2. Grace and peace come from the unity of the Father and the Son. This reminds us that the unity of the Church (and all human love and fellowship) ultimately flows out of the Living God who is a unity! The Father, Son and Holy Spirit have been perfectly united together in love and purpose for infinite ages before the universe began.

We can never claim to be a healthy or truthful church if we are not united in our gospel work together.

It is important that Paul calls the Philippian Christians "saints" – "holy ones". The Hebrew Scriptures define Israel as the LORD's *holy people*. For example, when the Angel of the LORD brings Moses and the people to Mt Sinai in Exodus 19, the first words that the LORD speaks from the mountain define Israel as a holy people.

> **Exodus 19:5-6** "Out of all nations you will be my treasured possession. Although the whole earth is mine, you will be for me a kingdom of priests and a holy nation. These are the words you are to speak to the Israelites."

As we go through Philippians we will see that there was a problem with unbelievers who wanted to enforce the Law on the Philippian believers. By addressing them as 'the holy ones' Paul is acknowledging that whatever the false teachers say, the Philippians are members of the LORD's holy nation. This will become very important when we begin to study chapter 3.

2. I HAVE YOU IN MY HEART (3-8)

Verse 3 poses a slight problem. In the NIV translation of the Bible it reads "I thank my God every time I remember you", but it could equally well be translated "I thank my God every time *you* remember *me*." [4]

The second option is perhaps slightly more likely, because of the way that it leads into the next verse. Paul thanks the Father every time the Philippians think about *him*, and he wants *them* to know how he remembers *them* in his prayers all the time.

---

[4] The Greek is literally – "every remembrance of me". Does that mean 'every time I remember' or 'every time I am remembered'?

We know that the Philippians have been thinking about Paul's gospel work because they have sent him money. In 4:15-16 Paul describes how they kept giving money to him while he was in Thessalonica.

> **Philippians 4:15-16** "…as you Philippians know, in the early days of your acquaintance with the gospel, when I set out from Macedonia, not one church shared with me in the matter of giving and receiving, *except you only*; for even when I was in Thessalonica, you sent me aid again and again when I was in need."

Given that he was only in Thessalonica for about a month, it shows how passionate the Philippian church was towards him. So, it makes sense that Paul would acknowledge their generosity at the beginning of the letter, as well as his proper 'thank you' at the end.

So, Paul is full of joy because he knows that the Philippians are fully behind him in his evangelism. When we are facing fierce opposition from the world and false teachers, nothing is as precious to us as genuine, practical fellowship with other gospel-centred Christians. When we speak about the need for "Christian fellowship" or the "lack of community" in the church, what are we really looking for? It is not just a matter of having a cup of tea after a Sunday service. We need to be 'gospel-partners' together, sharing our lives as we put the mission of Jesus ahead of everything in life. It is when we are serving each other in the service of Jesus that we find genuine fellowship.

Hugh Palmer, the minister of All Souls church in London, points out that every person we meet needs to be a gospel partner. If we meet a non-Christian person, our desire is not just that they be saved from hell, but that they become a gospel-partner in the church in this life. The gospel sets us free from a wasted life now and sets us free from hell in the future.

Paul uses the Greek word '*koinonia*' (English – 'partnership') to speak of the way the Philippian Christians are joined with him in the gospel work. This is the word that later Christians used to describe the way in which the Father, Son and Holy Spirit are united together.[5] The Philippians share their lives (and money) with Paul in the work of the gospel.

---

[5] Although no-one in the Bible uses the word to describe the Trinity, it seems a reasonable word to summarise all that Jesus says about the Trinity in John 17, for example.

Paul points out that 'from the first day' the Philippians were like this. This was a very clear mark that the Father was genuinely at work in them. We all come across those who appear to begin the Christian life, but they are reluctant to be sacrificial gospel-partners. This naturally makes us hesitant about their true spiritual state. Paul had no such hesitations with the Philippians. He was confident that the Father had begun the work of salvation in them (verse 6) and would certainly complete it, so that on the day when Jesus returns they would be welcomed into the New Creation.

There is such warm affection in these opening verses and Paul explains why he feels like that. "I have you in my heart" (verse 7) shows us the deep love that the apostle has for them.

Why does he love them in this way?

- the Philippians share in God's grace with Paul (verse 7);
- and the love of Jesus flows through him to them (verse 8).

Verse 7 – while Paul is in prison his apostolic ministry is limited, but when he is out of prison he "defends" and "confirms" the gospel. Paul *defended* the gospel from false teaching from within and criticism from outside. He also *confirmed* the gospel in preaching as a witness appointed by Jesus. We see this kind of language in Hebrews 2:3-4 – "This salvation, which was first announced by the Lord, was *confirmed* to us by those who heard him. God also testified to it by signs, wonders and various miracles, and gifts of the Holy Spirit distributed according to his will."[6]

So, as an apostle, Paul was establishing the gospel wherever he could... and the Philippians shared with him in this. The "grace of God" in verse 7 could refer to this apostolic work, but also to the fact that both Paul and the Philippians were united in the grace of God in the gospel. The apostle and the saints all stand together in the undeserved friendship of the Living God.

In verse 8 Paul calls the Father as a witness of how much he longs to be with the Philippians, but the love that Paul feels is not of his own making. Paul is so joined to Jesus, so in harmony with the mind and heart and agenda of Jesus, that he loves the Philippians with the love of Jesus.

Too often Paul is caricatured as simply a tough-minded debater, yet in these opening verses we are shown the true heart of the great apostle. He was a man whose life was Jesus. His heart was beating in time with Jesus' heart. Jesus love for the Church flowed through Paul.

---

6 See also Acts 14:3

Paul is studied by thousands of scholars around the world for the content of his mind, and yet we must also study the content of his heart.

We must not only agree with the *doctrine* of Paul but also the *love* of Paul, drawn from the love of Jesus Himself.

3. THIS IS MY PRAYER (9-11)

Paul made it clear that he often prayed for the Philippians. What did he pray for them? That is what he explains in these verses.

We saw the great love in Paul's heart, so we are not surprised to see that it is the great theme of his prayer. We can break the prayer up to understand what he is saying.

> that your *love* may abound more and more
> in knowledge and depth of insight,
> *so that*
> you may be able to discern what is best
> and may be pure and blameless until the day of Christ,
> filled with the fruit of righteousness that comes through Jesus Christ —
> to the glory and praise of God.

Paul asked for *love* for the Philippian church. That tells us right away what this letter is going to be about — love between the saints at Philippi.

It is not as if they don't have love already. If their love must "abound *more*", then it indicates that their love already abounds! We have seen evidence of that in their generosity in supporting Paul. However, perhaps Paul is asking that their love abound more and more *with knowledge and insight*. He wants the Father to grant them knowledge and insight so that their love could be focused more fruitfully.

The connection between love and knowledge is always in Paul's mind. In Romans 14 he explains how knowledge in eating practices must be controlled by love. In 1 Corinthians 13, in his great exposition of love, he begins by stating that all knowledge without love is *nothing*. In those cases, knowledge must be controlled by love, but here he wants the Philippians' love to be informed by knowledge. Their love is evident in their support for the gospel, but is it being lived out as it should in their local church fellowship? They need to understand more about what the love of Jesus looks like in the Church family.

One of the mistakes I have made is thinking that the love shown in evangelism is more real than day-to-day church family love. This letter shows us that we need a fully informed love, a love for the lost and for the saved, a love for souls and bodies.

Paul's request for a "knowledgeable love" is for a purpose (verse 10). Knowledgeable love would make them able to test and discern the best way for them to live. This, in turn, would have two results: the glory of God; and their purity and fruitfulness when they stand before Jesus on the Last Day. In 2:14 he will show that 'purity' involves "doing everything without complaining or arguing".

In 2 Timothy we see how Paul had a great passion for Christian fruitfulness. The Christian might make bad, worldly choices and end up 'ashamed' before Jesus. So, the Christian must keep their eyes on the future, making the right (though costly) choices now, so that they will be unashamed and fruitful before Jesus. One of the key things that Paul is doing in this letter is instructing the Philippians (and us) exactly what is "the best" way to live. What way of life will unite the church family together? What purpose can unite our minds and hearts, leading us into the joy, contentment and love that are in Jesus? What is "the best" that will ensure that we are profitable, fruit-bearing servants of Jesus?

This is what Paul wants for the Philippians. He wants them to be full of righteous fruit, produced by Jesus through them, when they enter into the New Creation.

Paul's prayer has such depth. We learn so much truth as he allows us to listen in on his prayers for the Philippians.

As we study this letter together, let's take Paul's prayer for ourselves and our own church family. We must abound in love, and this love must be guided and directed by the deep insights that the Bible will show us as we study it. In this way our local church family will be full of righteous fruit and we need have no shame when the Lord Jesus gazes upon us with his flaming eyes on that Last Day.

SUGGESTED QUESTIONS FOR BIBLE STUDY ON
PHILIPPIANS 1:1-11

1. To which members of the church do Paul and Timothy write according to verse 1? What might this tell us about Paul's thinking as he writes?

2. Who are the "saints" of verse 1 (compare Exodus 19:5-6)?

    What difference does it make to be referred to as a saint?

3. What does Paul mean when he speaks of the Philippians' "partnership in the gospel"? In what ways have they demonstrated this partnership?

4. How does Paul describe the way he prays for the Philippians in verses 4-6?

5. Why could Paul speak with such confidence about the future of the saints at Philippi in verse 6?

6. Why does Paul have such affection for the believers at Philippi?

    What lessons might we learn concerning our attitude to other believers from this verse? How do we "share in God's grace"?

7. What is the specific request of Paul in his prayer to God for the Philippians in verse 9?

    What will be the effect of this prayer according to verses 10 and 11?

8. What might be the effect on our church if we prayed as Paul does in verses 9-11?

2. Live as a citizen worthy of the gospel of Christ. 1:12-30

'Paul ministering in chains'

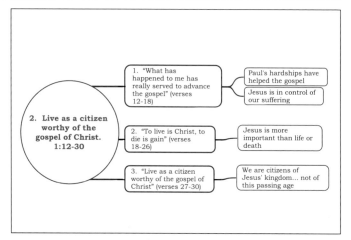

1. "WHAT HAS HAPPENED TO ME HAS REALLY SERVED TO ADVANCE THE GOSPEL" (VERSES 12-18)

The Philippian church has shown great love for Paul and they must have been very worried about him. In verse 26 we see how overjoyed they would be to see Paul again. However, Paul is in prison and could lose his life at any time. The great preacher of the 4th century AD, John Chrysostom, says that Paul knew that the Philippians were very anxious about him so he wanted to give them reassurance at the beginning of the letter. He didn't want them worrying about him.

"I want you to know" (verse 12). Paul gets to the issue right away. He explains that his imprisonment is not a problem but a great opportunity for the gospel.

If we were in prison and our Christian friends asked us how we were doing, what would we say? Perhaps we might say, "Yes, I'm doing quite well. The prison is quite uncomfortable, but the food is not as bad as you might expect. I've managed to get a warm blanket, but I am suffering from a bad chest. I've managed to make a few friends and my court case is going quite well. I have a good lawyer who has thought of a way of conducting my defence… etc." That is the normal way of human thinking. However, the apostle Paul is so completely absorbed with Jesus and the gospel that his own little story is not worth mentioning compared to the great gospel of Jesus. Paul views his own life only in terms of the gospel of Jesus.

> "To the question how it is with *him* an apostle *must* react with information as to how it is with the *Gospel*." [7]

By being in prison in Rome, at the centre of the empire, he has been able to get the gospel into the palace. In verse 13 he tells us the amazing fact that the gospel has become *clear* to "the whole palace guard". In fact, not only the guards, but 'everyone else' can see that Paul is not in prison because of any crimes he has committed, but simply because he is a servant of Jesus Christ.

The Philippians (and all of us) need to know that Christian suffering is not a disaster but, by the power of Jesus, a great opportunity. When we are weak, then we are strong, if we are drawing our strength only from the Father, Son and Holy Spirit.

In verses 14-17 we see how the Christians in Rome reacted to Paul's imprisonment. The two reactions shown reveal whether people have understood Christian suffering.

In verse 14 Paul speaks of *most* of the Christians who have reacted with maturity to Paul's imprisonment. They have seen how Jesus has been able to make the gospel clear to so many through Paul's situation. This has made them even more passionate and committed in their own evangelism. They saw that they had nothing to fear. Even if they too end up in prison or became martyrs, nevertheless the gospel of Jesus can be advanced through them too.

The enemies of the gospel probably assumed that Paul's imprisonment would have intimidated the other Christians, making them fearful of speaking about the gospel. However, we do not fear what they fear. For the unbeliever, death is very frightening because they have no real hope for the future. For the Christian, the greatest fear is living an unfruitful life, a life that dishonours Jesus. We do not fear death, because it is simply the time when we go to wait for the New Creation *with Jesus*. So, Paul's example of faithfulness to the gospel helped most of the Christians in Rome to live faithfully too.

---

[7] Karl Barth, *The Epistle to the Philippians*, SCM, London, 1962, page 26.

Once more they venture further forward than they have evidently done for a time. The Word spoken in their midst through the imprisonment of the apostle has awakened in them, too, the old insight that 'Christianity' is no private business but a matter of thoroughly and specifically public concern, and must also be represented by 'Christians' as such. The light, the movement, the power that proceeded from the prisoners' testimony has automatically put the Word of God once more on their lips as well, and made them employ their freedom more fearlessly than ever amid the indifference of the metropolis and its hostility to the truth. That is the other thing in which Paul sees the advance of the Gospel in Rome. [8]

The gospel has advanced... as unbelievers were saved *and* as Christians were encouraged to speak out.

However, *some* (verse 15) were not like that. They were envious of Paul and saw themselves as rivals. They presumably thought that with Paul out of the way in prison, they would be able to get a strong following for themselves by preaching the gospel. In verse 17 we see that they were preaching the gospel of Christ out of selfish ambition – wanting to become famous preachers or revered leaders. In fact, they want to "stir up trouble" for Paul while he is in prison. This seems to indicate that they were actually trying to turn the Church away from Paul. Perhaps they were saying, "Paul is not worth bothering about anymore. He obviously wasn't such a great apostle because he has ended up locked away in prison. Is *that* a sign of Christ's blessing? Forget Paul and I will tell you about Christ."[9]

It is important that we see how Paul handles this situation. He has no personal pride at all. He realises that these misguided 'brothers' were not preaching heresy. They *were* preaching *Christ*, even if their motives were mixed with selfish ambition. Remember in Galatians how fierce Paul was towards those who preach 'another' Christ who is no Christ at all. Here, the situation is quite different. The real Jesus is being preached and Paul is full of joy about that even though these 'brothers' were causing harm and heartache for Paul.

---

[8] Barth, 28

[9] Some have wondered if these envious preachers were unbelievers who were stirring up trouble for Paul by preaching about Christ to the Roman authorities, trying to enflame the situation for Paul. This view was held by the great Chrysostom, but it may not be the best explanation.

Would you be so self-sacrificial, so focused only on the glory of Jesus? If a gospel-preaching brother was unjustly causing you harm or speaking against you, what would your reaction be? Would you leap to your own defence? Would you retaliate against that brother? Would you defend all this with pious words? We need to study how Paul behaved. His life and reputation were of no concern at all, so long as the gospel of Jesus was being advanced.

As we look back at the situation it is hard for us to imagine how Christians could fail to love the apostle Paul. We see the apostle at a safe distance, full of admiration at how he poured out his life for Jesus. However in his day his challenge could not be kept at arms length in the way that we might be able to do. When Paul visited a church or wrote to a church his great love (for Jesus and for people) meant that he was not prepared to be silent or passive when he saw compromise or sin or division. Paul exposed the darkness in the churches and, through both his life and teaching, drove the Christians to faithful suffering, bold witness and joy unspeakable in fellowship with Jesus by the Holy Spirit. The Christians would have either loved him deeply or recoiled from him as he destroyed their 'comfort zone'. Today it is easy to *say* that we love Paul while living in a way that Paul would have radically challenged. Back then, in his company, such hypocrisy would have been much harder to hide.

2. "TO LIVE IS CHRIST, TO DIE IS GAIN" (VERSES 18-26)

Paul is full of joy... even in prison, even when harmed by divisive 'brothers'. His knows such joy because Jesus means everything to him.

In these next verses *that* is the great truth that we need to learn from Paul. Whatever difficulties and opposition and misunderstanding we each face, we can not only endure but live with great joy if we set aside our personal 'life' and accept the *life* of Jesus as our *true* life.

The constant tendency of the fallen human mind and heart is to assume that giving ourselves to Jesus will be bad for us. We constantly assume that we will be happiest and most fulfilled if we look after our own interests. *That* is what went so dreadfully wrong in the Garden of Eden with Adam and Eve. They listened to Lucifer's suggestion that Jesus was keeping true joy from them. They learned the hard way that the life of Jesus is true life and joy and fulfilment and freedom. We are all suffering that lesson today, yet how many of us have really learned the lesson as the apostle Paul did?

We begin at the end of verse 18 – "Yes, and I will continue to rejoice *for…*" Paul has two reasons to explain his ongoing joy: the prayers of the Philippians and the help of the Holy Spirit. The fact that Paul mentions their prayer even though he is assured of the help of the Spirit seems amazing to us.

What are *human* prayers compared to the work of the Spirit? This reminds us of the power of prayer. When a church prays in unity then our Almighty Father will listen. *We* are powerless, but in the Father, Son and Holy Spirit is power and authority beyond our wildest imagination. When we acknowledge our utter dependence on the gracious care of our heavenly Father and turn to Him in sincere prayer, He loves to grant our requests. Jesus was completely serious when He said that whatever we ask in His Name will be given to us (John 14:13-14). The tragedy is that we pray so little and so many of our prayers are in our own name, for our own convenience and desires. The apostle is full of joy because he knows that the wisdom and resources of the Father are released to him through the prayers of the Philippians.

However, Paul receives help not only from the Father, but also "the help given by the Spirit of Jesus Christ" (verse 19). It is no accident that Paul relates the Holy Spirit to Jesus here. We see *the whole Trinity* mobilised to help the apostle Paul in the heart of Rome. The Roman empire didn't stand a chance!

Paul separates the prayers of the Philippians from the help of the Spirit perhaps because he knows that even if all the churches turned against him, yet the Holy Spirit never would. Even if nobody prayed for him, yet he would still know the joy of the Spirit's fellowship. Romans 8:26 – "the Spirit himself intercedes for us with groans that words cannot express".

At the end of verse 19 Paul quotes from Job 13:16. This "will turn out for my deliverance."

In Job chapter 11, Zophar stupidly suggested that the only way for Job to escape God's judgement was to work hard to make himself better. Job rejects this heresy and in chapter 13 he explains that he trusts in the Lord whatever happens to him. He is completely sure that he is accepted by the Lord God and that he will stand in His presence after he dies.

Why do I put myself in jeopardy and take my life in my hands? Though he slay me, yet will I hope in him; I will surely defend my ways to his face. Indeed, this will turn out for my deliverance.

It is important for us to see the original context of this quotation so that we understand what Paul is really saying. Some people have assumed that Paul simply means that by the prayers of the Philippians and the help of the Spirit he *will get out of his Roman prison*. However, when we see what Job was saying, and what Paul goes on to say, we see that Paul is not thinking like that at all.

Like Job, what is on Paul's mind is how he will stand before the Lord Jesus *after death*. Paul knows that he will not be sent to Hell, but he does not want to be "ashamed" when he meets Jesus. Paul wants to live a life of fruitful service for Jesus and to be greeted with the words "well done, good and faithful servant." The exaltation of Jesus is the great goal of his life... and failure at that point is unbearable for Paul.

The 'deliverance' that Paul is confident of is being delivered from a wasted or barren life that does not glorify Jesus.

In verse 20 he explains that he is full of excitement knowing that whether he is killed by the Romans or allowed to live for a while longer, yet "Christ will be exalted in my body." The circumstances of his own bodily life, whether in prison or free, whether healthy of sick, whether rich or poor, can all be endured with great joy so long as Christ is being exalted through it all.

The glory of Jesus is far, far more important than life and death, and if we are sure that our life and death will exalt Jesus then true peace and joy are ours.

Paul wants courage (verse 20). His only concern is that in his human weakness, through all the opposition and persecution, he will lack the courage to hold firm to Jesus. However, he was full of expectation and hope that, with the prayers of the Philippians and the help of the Spirit, he would be delivered from betraying Jesus.

Verse 21 is one of the greatest verses in the whole Bible. "For to me, to live is Christ and to die is gain." The only life that Paul is concerned about is the eternal life that he has in Jesus. The temporary bodily 'life' of the present is eclipsed by the everlasting life that is the life of Jesus. The life of Jesus carries us through death to heaven and beyond to bodily life in the New Creation. To "lose" the bodily life of this present time is no loss at all, because when we are absent from the body we are in the immediate presence of Jesus waiting in Paradise. To lose our temporary bodily life is to experience more deeply our true life, the life of Jesus. Thus, death is gain, for anyone with Jesus' life.

The test of our Christian maturity is our ability to confess Philippians 1:21.

Life in the body (verse 22) is simply more time to be fruitful for Jesus, more time to exalt Him and advance His gospel. Paul feels himself torn between the choice between life and death. If it was simply his own choice, considered from his own interests, he would choose death. Death would mean going to be directly with Jesus in paradise. Being with Jesus is so wonderful, so glorious, that nothing in this passing age compares to *that* (verse 23). However, as always, Paul does not put his own interests first (verse 24). He feels that he must remain a little longer in the body for the *benefit of the church*. The Lord Jesus still has more for him to do in the service of the church so Paul must put his own interests aside and continue living for a while.

Paul's attitude seems so far from the materialism and worldliness that so easily seeps into our hearts and minds. When we think of what we most want, how many of us would say with Paul, "to die and be with Jesus"?

When we *think* like Paul we will also *live* like Paul and *change the world for Jesus* like Paul.

Verses 25-26 must have been comforting to the Philippians. They dearly loved Paul and would have found it very hard to lose his wisdom and love. For their *progress* and *joy in the faith* he would remain. They would overflow with joy when he came to visit them again.

3. "LIVE AS A CITIZEN WORTHY OF THE GOSPEL OF CHRIST" (VERSES 27-30)

Chapter 1:27-28 is a kind of summary of the whole letter. If we are going to learn any verses from this letter, then these are the ones. In fact, these verses are a kind of plan for the rest of the letter. Paul writes this letter to show the Philippians how to do what he describes in verses 27-28.

As we noted in the introduction, the city of Philippi treasured its status within the Roman empire. Acts 16 presents us with a city that valued Roman citizenship all too highly. It is vital that we translate 1:27 correctly so that we understand how Paul begins to challenge this culture of worldly citizenship.

"Live as a citizen worthy of the gospel of Christ."

The verse begins with the Greek word *monon*, which means "only". Barth suggests that we translate it "Just one thing…".[10] After taking the Philippians to the heights of verses 20-21 and contemplating his own future, he seems to 'hold up his finger' to speak to them about what their future needed to look like.

Whether Paul manages to visit them again or is kept in prison, the most important thing for the Philippian church is that…

1. They are united – standing firm in *one* Spirit, contending as one man, serving one another.

2. They are focused on the gospel – contending for the faith of the gospel.

3. They are not frightened by opposition – without being frightened in any way by those who oppose you.

It is easy to see how these concerns have been shown by Paul in all that he has said so far. He tried to maintain unity with those who preach the gospel, even though they are not standing with him. His only ambition in life is that the gospel would advance and he constantly seeks opportunities to tell others. He is confident that he will be given the courage to be faithful in the face of so much dangerous opposition. He does not fear death at all, but longs to be with Christ.

Is Paul speaking about the Holy Spirit here or, as most of the translators assume, 'a spirit of unity'? When we remember other Scriptures then it seems clear that Paul is here thinking of the Holy Spirit: Ephesians 2:18 "For through (Jesus) we both have access to the Father by one Spirit" or Ephesians 4:1-4 "As a prisoner for the Lord, then, I urge you to live a life worthy of the calling you have received. Be completely humble and gentle; be patient, bearing with one another in love. Make every effort to keep the unity of the Spirit through the bond of peace. There is one body and one Spirit—just as you were called to one hope when you were called" or 1 Corinthians 12:13 "we were all baptised by one Spirit into one body – whether Jews or Greeks, slave or free – and we were all given the one Spirit to drink".

The Holy Spirit unites all believers into one Body. It is not something that we need to achieve, but is a gift and a fact of our life in Jesus. The key challenge is that the way we live together must not be a denial of what we really are in the Holy Spirit.

---

[10] Barth, page 45.

In the Greek, Paul doesn't say "contending as one *man*", but "contending as one *soul/mind*". Having a single *mind* is the great challenge of Christian unity. With all the different denominations and cultures and opinions and emphases, how can we ever have *one mind*?

The key is that we have one mind as *we contend for the faith of the gospel*.

The Bible is more like a wilderness survival guide than a theoretical textbook. The Bible is equipping us to trust in Jesus the Messiah in this passing age, fighting against the world, the flesh and the devil. When *that* captures our hearts and minds it is amazing how the relatively tiny differences between all true believers melt away. All genuine believers share "the faith of the gospel" which sets them all apart from the world by a huge chasm. What too often happens is that we spend too much time focusing on the differences between us and not enough time on dealing with the world, the flesh and the devil.

For several years, my wife Liz and I used to go each week to Speaker's Corner in London where we tried to preach the gospel with a small but very diverse group of Christians. We were Anglican, Methodist, Baptist, Brethren, Pentecostal, house church and who knows what else... and yet the experience of unity and love between us was amazing. Trying to 'sort each other out' on all kinds of non-gospel matters was far from our minds. This is not to say that theology and Bible truth were not important. It was a time of deep theological study and learning, but all of our effort and work was focused on the simple goal of exalting Christ each week in a situation of severe opposition. Over time, as we matured in that context, we all drew closer together on so many theological issues, but that was never the focus of our attention.

Paul doesn't say "get one mind together *and then* contend for the faith of the gospel". *That* could just lead to argument and division. No, he tells us the proper way for us to get one mind together. When we recognise our gospel task, then we see how much we desperately need each other in the work... and we get our priorities in order. Facing secularism, unbelief, other religious systems, worldliness and false teaching requires all our energy.

The gospel itself defines our common mind.

If our minds are full of the gospel of Jesus, focused on advancing that gospel in all we do, then we find that we are in full agreement with all the other believers who are doing the same.

If our church is inward looking, focused merely on maintaining our own purity or serving our own needs, then our church will be divisive and disconnected from the Christian family.

Notice that Paul does not say "fight together *against*... unbelief, the world, the Roman empire, declining moral standards etc." Rather we fight *for* the faith of the gospel. Again, it is not that we fight for *our own faith*, as if we were fighting to maintain our own position. No! We contend for the faith of the gospel. We are fighting for the advance of the gospel, for the honour of Jesus. The goal is not the *defeat* of something but the *triumph* of Jesus.

Verse 28 makes it clear that Paul is focusing our attention on the big issues of eternity in order to unite us together. Judgement day is coming – salvation and damnation are ultimate matters. Our future is one of indescribable hope – an everlasting life with Jesus, in Paradise and then into the renewed creation. For us death is *gain*. For the unbelieving world, death is frightening and leads to Hades, where they await the final judgement in terror.

The fact that we stand *together* without fear of the future even when the world opposes us and threatens us reveals this stark truth. The world fixes its hope on *this* world and is very fearful of death and the future because this age is passing away. The way that Christians experience joy and peace even in the most severe suffering and opposition is one of the clearest demonstrations of the truth of the gospel. It shows that we are in the hands of the Living God, who will certainly save us from the coming judgement if He is holding us so firm through the trials of this passing age.

Verses 29-30 are so different to the attitude of a worldly Christianity. When Paul was in Philippi he experienced intense opposition, as recorded in Acts 16. The Philippian Church was going through the same kind of trouble. Now, instead of complaining about this, Paul sees it as a sign of special divine favour on the Philippian Christians!

The worldly minded person might have been tempted to moan: "Oh, dear, I'm so sorry that you have ended up in the same trouble that I had. God must be angry at us. Let's pray that He blesses us by giving us lots of peace and quiet and an easy life."

Paul sees through the attitudes of the flesh and sees the wonderful spiritual reality of life with Jesus. "It has been granted to you on behalf of Christ not only to believe on Him, but also to suffer for Him." A king "*grants*" favours and privileges. Paul sees suffering opposition for Jesus as a special privilege or favour granted by the Father. It is the experience of so many of us that in the heart-ache and pain of persecution and suffering comes the most wonderful, sweet fellowship with Jesus. When we are allowed to walk the way of the Cross with Him we find ourselves drawn very close to Him. If things are hard for us then we are overjoyed that glory is going to Jesus. If being close to Jesus is more than life and death to us, then we understand why Paul saw this as a privilege rather than a curse.

SUGGESTED QUESTIONS FOR 'LIVE AS A CITIZEN WORTHY OF THE GOSPEL OF CHRIST'. 1:12-30

1. How does Paul view his imprisonment?

   What does he have to say in these verses about his own condition and treatment whilst in prison?

   What might we be able to learn for the times when we are in great difficulties?

2. What are the two reactions to Paul's imprisonment as described in verses 14-17?

   What is surprising about both of them?

3. What is Paul's attitude to those who cause him trouble but still teach people about Jesus?

4. What does Paul mean by "deliverance" in verse 19? Read Job 13:15-16 and verse 20.

   How does this help us to understand Paul's motives in these verses?

5. What does Paul need courage for in his situation? Verse 20.

6. Does Paul's attitude to life and death in verse 21 differ from our own?

7. How does Paul demonstrate his love and concern for the Philippians in verses 24-26?

8. Read Acts 16:35-39. What do these verses tell us about the way the people of Philippi view Roman citizenship?

   What difference would verse 27 make in Phillipi?

9. What three things does Paul want the Philippian church to be doing according to verses 27-28?

   What would these things look like in our own circumstances?

10. Why does Paul describe gospel work as "contending"?

11. How is living without fear in gospel work a sign of the future? Verse 28.

12. What is Paul's attitude to the sufferings that the Philippian church is going through? Verses 29-30.

3. Your attitude should be the same as that of Christ Jesus. 2:1-11

'Jesus the servant who is God'

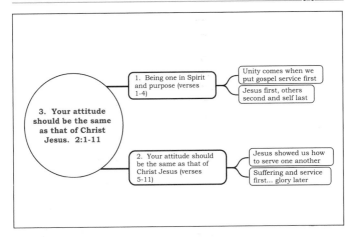

1. BEING ONE IN SPIRIT AND PURPOSE (VERSES 1-4)

Remember chapter 1:27-28.

1:27-28a "Whatever happens, *live as a citizen worthy of the gospel of Christ*. Then, whether I come and see you or only hear about you in my absence, I will know that you *stand firm in one Spirit*, contending as one man *(with one mind)* for the faith of the gospel without being frightened in any way by those who oppose you."

We will see how Paul now unpacks these verses throughout the rest of the epistle. In the section we are examining now (2:1-11) he shows how we must *"stand firm in one Spirit"*. In the next section he will show us how to contend "as one man for the faith of the gospel".

In verse 1 Paul loads up all the benefits that we have in Jesus – encouragement, comfort, fellowship, tenderness and compassion.

If we are suffering for Jesus, then we are also encouraged and comforted by Jesus. The world and the enemies of the gospel may try to discourage us but the comfort of Jesus is so very much greater. They may try to take away our peace, but we have divine comfort. We know the fellowship of the Spirit even if we are rejected by the world. If the enemies of Jesus show us no mercy or love, yet Jesus treats us with great tenderness and compassion.

When Paul puts "if any" at the beginning of each clause, he is expecting us to respond with an exclamation of how much we have in Jesus. Do we have any encouragement from being united to Jesus? YES! We have lots and lots! Do we have *any* comfort from His infinite love? YES! We are wonderfully comforted even in the most uncomfortable situations. It is as if someone might say, "If the North Pole is cold; if the Sahara desert is dry; if the Atlantic Ocean is wet; if the sun is hot…"

Because there are so many of these benefits in Jesus, (verse 2) then the Philippians should be able to be united together in love. The disunity of the Philippian church is the one thing that concerns Paul about them. He knows that they love him very much, that they show their support for the gospel through their wallets, that they are blessed in being considered worthy of suffering for Jesus… and yet, the division among them is a serious problem.

The support that we have in Jesus not only helps us when the world opposes us, it also means that we do not need to be demanding or unforgiving within the Church family.

We are strengthened to think the best of one another and overlook the weaknesses of each other. If fellow Christians discourage us, then we will find all the encouragement we need in Jesus. We don't need to retaliate or carry grudges. If we are hurt by the thoughtlessness of our brothers and sisters, then the God of all comfort will comfort us. The fellowship of the Holy Spirit means that we are never alone. When others forget us, the Spirit never will. If we don't receive the tenderness and compassion that we need from others, Jesus the Good Shepherd will always treat us gently. In my own experience, when other Christians have caused me hurt, Jesus will always provide so much more comfort and encouragement than I can ever get by holding a grudge. Love covers over many sins (Proverbs 10:12; 1 Peter 4:8). I am able to love my brothers and sisters in this gracious way only when I find my security and stability and strength in Jesus.

Paul describes the unity that he wants for them in a list:

- like-minded
- having the same love
- being one in Spirit
- being one in purpose

Like-minded. We saw in 1:27 that our common mind must be defined by the gospel itself. In 2:12-18 Paul will conclude all that he has said in verses 1-11 with a description of the Philippians engaged in evangelism.

When Richard Bewes and I went to the Billy Graham evangelists' conference in Amsterdam in 2000, we were amazed at the unity that the gospel brings. People from every culture, speaking every language, from all kinds of church situations gathered for one purpose: how can we take the gospel of Jesus to the world? Because our minds and hearts were united by *that* great task, we found ourselves sharing a common mind beyond all the superficial differences of nation, language, denomination and culture.

The church can be like-minded only under the banner of the gospel of Jesus.

In 1 Corinthians 1:10 Paul makes a similar appeal to the Corinthian church: "I appeal to you, brothers, in the name of our Lord Jesus Christ, that all of you agree with one another so that there may be no divisions among you and that *you may be perfectly united in mind and thought*." In the following chapters Paul will show them the futility of human thinking. He drives them back to the Bible alone for all their thinking – (1 Corinthians 4:6 – "do not go beyond what is written"). However, Paul's starting point in 1 Corinthians 1 is the preaching of the gospel – (1 Corinthians 1:23-24 – "we preach Christ crucified: a stumbling-block to Jews and foolishness to Gentiles, but to those whom God has called, both Jews and Greeks, Christ the power of God and the wisdom of God." [11])

Many Christians find the widespread disunity among Christians terribly disheartening. The apostle Paul seems to have been such a Christian. Some of us might be tempted to give up and resign ourselves to constant division. The apostle Paul had the answer. We can have one mind if our minds are fixed on the gospel. The Church is on the earth with one great mission to fulfil – to preach the gospel to everyone. Our gaze needs to be fixed on that great commission that Jesus left us with (Matthew 28:18-20 – "Jesus came to them and said, 'All authority in heaven and on earth has been given to me.

---

[11] Even our study of the Bible will not free us from division unless we are studying the Bible with humility and gospel passion. The Bible was written to equip the Church for the gospel-mission given to her. If it is studied out of intellectual pride or merely academic curiosity, then its message will be hidden and division is inevitable.

Therefore go and make disciples of all nations, baptising them in the name of the Father and of the Son and of the Holy Spirit, and teaching them to obey everything I have commanded you. And surely I am with you always, to the very end of the age.'"). If our gaze wanders from *that* onto all kinds of other questions and agenda (however worthy and interesting they may be), then division follows as surely as night follows day.

It is worth noting that attempts at church unity that are based on other ideas or strategies are doomed to failure. Unity without a common gospel-focused mind is no unity at all. When people hold to a false gospel then we can never be "like-minded" with them.

Having the same love. What does the word 'same' mean here? Should the Philippians love each other with the same love that Paul has for them or that they have for Paul? It is more likely that they should love each other with the same love that *Jesus* has for them that Paul mentioned in verse 1. Remember what Paul said in 1:8 – "God can testify how I long for all of you with the affection of Christ Jesus." Now he wants them to have that same love for each other, the love that Jesus has for them.

This is an excellent place to start. First, we don't need to worry about our own sinful feelings. The love of Jesus is the standard and the source. As we draw near to Him so He fills our hearts with His own love. Second, Jesus has shown us what His real love looks like. His love is not mere sentiment but practical and useful. He gave up His own interests and benefits in order to help us. *That* is how we are to love each other with Jesus' love. The question is not "do I feel warm feelings towards everyone in my church family?", but "what am I *doing* to love and serve them?"

Being one in the Spirit. Paul returns to one of his favourite themes: the unity that we already have in the Holy Spirit. It is vital for us to always remember that the unity of the Church is already true and real before we do anything. We are already the one Body of Jesus, joined together by the Holy Spirit. Church unity is not a goal for us to achieve, but a reality that we only have to express.

Being one in purpose. We have already seen the power of having the same purpose. When we all understand what our purpose is, then we can all gather together under the banner of the gospel. If some of us are pursuing worldly ambitions or materialistic goals then the church family will suffer. Our common gospel purpose is what draws us together, showing us how to use our gifts our money our opportunities. My worldliness and selfishness will damage the gospel unity of my church family.

In verses 3-4 Paul zooms in on the specific attitude that will make all this possible. Paul gets to the very root of the problem, and as he does this he shines the light of truth into all of us.

In the NIV translation, we get the phrase 'vain conceit' in verse 3, but this is not quite strong enough. The Greek word is *kenodoxia*. *Doxia* means 'glory', and you will notice how much Paul speaks of the glory of the Father and Jesus in this letter. For this reason we might better translate verse 3 as "Do nothing out of selfish ambition or *empty glory*, but in humility consider others better than yourselves."

This verse strikes at the very heart of all our sin and compromise, our unfaithfulness and division. It takes us right back to the Garden of Eden when, out of selfish ambition, Adam and Eve ate from the tree of the knowledge of good and evil. They desired for themselves what did not belong to them, what was forbidden to them. They put their own perceived interests ahead of the glory of their LORD. What they grasped was an *empty* glory.

All our actions and decisions must be motivated by the glory of Jesus and the Father. See how verses 5-11 arrive at the great crescendo of "to the glory of God the Father." In chapter 1:11 the aim of Paul's prayer was that on the day of Christ the Philippians would be fruitful "to the glory and praise of God." *That* is the only worthy ambition to govern our lives. If we are motivated by the *empty glory* of our own status, comfort or pleasure then we are not going the same way as the faithful Christians who are laying down their lives to the glory of God. If we use our time and resources out of selfish ambition then we will bring division into the church family. How can we be united in gospel witness with our brothers and sisters if we are motivated by such *empty glory* and selfish ambition?

"Selfish ambition" addresses the way we relate to our brothers and sisters in Jesus and "empty glory" looks vertically at how we live to the glory of the LORD Jesus and the Father.

The alternative is to "in humility consider others better than yourselves." How do we do this? It must begin with humility. In the Hebrew Scriptures, humility is the starting point before the LORD God.

Zephaniah 2:3 "Seek the LORD, all you humble of the land, you who do what he commands. Seek righteousness, seek humility; perhaps you will be sheltered on the day of the LORD's anger."

Before the LORD Jesus we must humble ourselves. All our boasting and self-confidence must be rejected as we bow before Him and trust in Him. As we humble ourselves before Him we see our true state. All the things that we might take pride in over others are worth nothing in His Presence. We are all poor sinners and all that we have is a sheer gracious gift from our generous Heavenly Father.

Think of the apostle Paul. He was a clever man, well-educated and well-travelled. He not only knew the Scriptures as very few have done, but he had also been taken to Paradise, experiencing things that he was not able to even speak about. For all that, how did he see himself?

1 Timothy 1:15-16 "Here is a trustworthy saying that deserves full acceptance: Christ Jesus came into the world to save sinners – *of whom I am the worst*. But for that very reason I was shown mercy so that in me, the worst of sinners, Christ Jesus might display his unlimited patience as an example for those who would believe on him and receive eternal life."

"Of whom I am the worst". Paul saw himself as the very worst sinner. All the wonderful advantages that he had enjoyed made his sin all the worse to him. Each one of us feels exactly the same as Paul as we stand before the Cross of Jesus. Each one of us feels that we are the very worst sinner. We know the corruption and hypocrisy in our own hearts. We know all the temptations and sins that fester within us. We all know the life we have lived… and we shudder. We feel amazed that the mercy of God extends even as far as us. This is what truly humbles us all.

In this humility we view others better than ourselves. It is not that we simply try to pick out ways in which others are better than us (although that is not a bad thing to do). It is rather seeing each one of us as objects of the unlimited grace of Jesus. We are to treat our brothers and sisters as they really are in Jesus.

Paul is not asking the impossible or the untrue, namely that I am to think that every other Christian, just because he is a Christian, has more brains, more ability, more everything than I have. Nor does Paul ask that we merely 'consider' one another above ourselves although we know that the facts are quite to the contrary, that a large number are far below us. *'As being above themselves' means as deserving first attention from us.* Romans 12:10 'In honour preferring one another'. Each is to put every other brother first on the list to be considered, himself at the bottom of the list; each one is to have the list arranged in this order. The worldling reverses this: *he* comes first, everyone else comes last, perhaps does not come at all. [12]

In verse 4 the NIV seems to suggest that it is right to look out for our own interests as long as we are also looking out for others – "not only... but also." However, this is not in the Greek. The verse simply says "each must not look after their own things, but the others' things."[13]

It is important that we understand this because this verse has been badly misused to promote self-interest! Some have claimed that this verse *tells* us to "look out for ourselves" so long as we *also* look out for others. This seems to be going in the opposite direction to the apostle Paul!

After telling us that we ought to place other believers above ourselves, he now shows what that looks like in very simple terms. Our concern must be for the needs of others rather than 'looking after number one'. The wonderful thing is that when we do that *together* in the church family we have no need to worry about our own needs because all the others will be doing that for us. It is such a great blessing when a fellow believer does something for us because they were concerned about our "interests", our "needs".

We should make it our business to look after the needs of others rather than ourselves.

2. YOUR ATTITUDE SHOULD BE THE SAME AS THAT OF CHRIST JESUS (VERSES 5-11)

In verse 2 we saw that the Philippians were to have the same love for each other as Jesus had for them, and now Paul calls for the same *mind* that Christ Jesus has. We find here the same word as we found in verse 2. We are to be *like-minded*, but the *mind* that we must all have is the *mind* of Jesus.

---

[12] Lenski, page 767

[13] In some Greek manuscripts there is the word which can be translated as 'also' – "each must not look

Of course, Paul is not concerned with how clever Jesus is, but with *the way that Jesus thinks*.

An ocean of ink and a forest of paper have been used to write about these 7 verses of Paul's letter. Many people have tried to uncover a complete 'theology of the incarnation' from these verses and long debates have raged about exactly what Paul means when he says that Jesus "made Himself nothing." We will give some attention to these matters, but it is vital that we understand the context of what Paul is writing.

Paul is NOT writing a theological paper about the technicalities of how Jesus became one of us. Paul is showing the Philippian church how to get on with each other. Verses 5-11 are intended to make us love and serve our fellow Christians... not develop theories of how Jesus was born of Mary!

Bishop Lightfoot, in his commentary, offers the following expanded translation:

> Reflect in your own minds the mind of Christ Jesus. Be humble, as He also was humble. Though existing before the worlds in the Eternal Godhead, yet He did not cling... to the prerogatives of His divine majesty, did not ambitiously display His equality with God; but divested Himself of the glories of heaven, and took upon Him the nature of a servant, assuming the likeness of men. Nor was this all. Having thus appeared among men in the fashion of a man, He humbled Himself yet more, and carried out His obedience even to dying. Nor did He die by a common death: He was crucified, as the lowest malefactor is crucified. But as was His humility, so also was His exaltation. God raised Him to a pre-eminent height, and gave Him a title and a dignity far above all dignities and titles else. For to the name and majesty of Jesus all created things in heaven and earth and hell shall pay homage on bended knee; and every tongue with praise and thanksgiving shall declare that Jesus Christ is Lord, and in and for Him shall glorify God the Father.

It may well be that 2:6-11 was a hymn used in the churches of Paul's day. If this is a hymn, it is quite possible that Paul himself wrote the hymn. Hymns are an excellent way of learning Biblical truth. For many of us, the truths of the Bible were absorbed through our hymns and songs before we ever formally studied the Bible.

The Living God is, and always has been, the Father, Son and Holy Spirit.[14] They are eternally, together, the One True God. Jesus is defined in this way for us in verse 6. He eternally existed in the Trinity, in the life of God.[15] Jesus shared the very same life as the Father and the Spirit before anything was created. We should compare this with Hebrews 1:3 – "The Son is the radiance of God's glory and the exact representation of His being."

That life of eternal glory and divine fellowship is Jesus' natural life. YET, He did not treat that life as something to be held in a tight grip (verse 6). He did not hold onto that glorious life as "a prize which must not slip from His grasp".[16] He did not say of that life, "this is mine and I will not let go of it. Enjoying this majestic glory is mine by right and I refuse to give that up."

Defining forever what true humility looks like, Jesus (verse 7) left the majestic glory of heaven behind and became like us. He emptied Himself of that majestic glory and took the very nature of a servant[17], becoming just like us earthly humans. From the world's perspective Jesus appeared to be nothing more than an ordinary man (verse 8).

Jesus *had* the "form" of God – that is to say, He not only was the Eternal LORD God, but it was manifestly obvious that He was. His appearance made it clear who He was. When people met the Eternal Son in the Old Testament, they knew that they had met with the LORD God. See Isaiah 6:1-5 for a very clear example.[18] However, Jesus was prepared to take the "form" of a servant, *appearing* to be just an ordinary man. He did not cease to be the Eternal Son when He became like us, yet He *did* leave behind the majesty and glory of heaven.

Jesus words in John 17:5 are very useful here: "And now, Father, glorify me in your presence with *the glory I had with you before the world began.*" In Jesus' prayer in John 17 He makes it clear that even without that glory, He is still

---

[14] See Lightfoot, *Saint Paul's Epistle to the Philippians*, (Macmillan, London, 1885) page 110 for an explanation of how Philippians 2:6 is matched by John 1:1.

[15] Lightfoot, page 110. See also 127-133. To be "in the form" *(morphe)* "is not the same as *fusis* or *ousia*, yet the possession of the *morphe* involves participation in the ousia also: for *morphe* implies not the external accidents but the essential attributes."

[16] Lightfoot, 111

[17] The same word *morphe* is used to describe the servant He became.

[18] See also John 12:41 for the confirmation that it was Jesus that Isaiah saw.

one with His Father. In John 5:18, even the enemies of Jesus acknowledged that He claimed to be "equal with God."

Paul does not say that Jesus became like a man but that He became like *humanity*. "The plural (humans) is used; for Christ, as the Second Adam, represents not the individual man, but the human race; Romans 5:15; 1 Corinthians 15:45-47." [19]

Paul's lesson in humility and self-sacrifice has already struck deeply into our thinking. In the church family the example and standard for our behaviour towards each other is clear. When we consider the privileges and blessings that we might enjoy, we must never treat them as things that must be selfishly hoarded up. If we are to be a united church family then we must be ready to give up all that we have for the good of others. "Who we are" is given to us in Jesus… and we can serve others without any loss of our identity or dignity.

Jesus set aside His own interests for the sake of the gospel… and if we all do the same then we will be united with a common mind, mutual love and the same purpose.

Acts 2:44-45 shows exactly what this "mind of Christ Jesus" looks like in church life. "All the believers were together and had everything in common. Selling their possessions and goods, they gave to anyone as he had need." We find the same thing at the end of Acts 4. "There were no needy persons among them. For from time to time those who owned lands or houses sold them, brought the money from the sales and put it at the apostles' feet, and it was distributed to anyone as he had need."

Paul has not finished his lesson though. Jesus did more than leave the glories of heaven. He humbled Himself still further, to the ultimate degree. He was obedient to the will of His Father, even though that took Him to death… and not just any death. He suffered the very worst death of all – "even death on a cross."

There were no limits to the way in which Jesus gave Himself for others. He did not say, "I will give up my privileges, but I will not give up my health, my life." He did not say, "I will leave behind the glories of heaven, but I will not be rejected by my Father." In the Garden of Gethsemane we see Him

[19] Lightfoot, 112

wrestling with this in agony. He had to release everything, to the ultimate degree, for the sake of others.

He kept nothing back, no matter how precious it was to Him.

We have seen that for everlasting ages Jesus had enjoyed the indescribable glory of the fellowship of the Father and the Spirit... but in Gethsemane He had to face the loss of even this. To lose what had been His most basic experience for eternal ages was so infinitely more costly than anything that we could ever have to give up. Our little privileges and status and possessions have only been enjoyed by us for a very few years. Yet, He humbled Himself in that infinite and ultimate way... to death on a cross.

To die on a cross has a much deeper significance in the Bible than it might have in the modern mind. Today, people acknowledge that such a death would have been very unpleasant, but I have even heard people suggest that there are other ways of dying that would be worse. This is to miss the point entirely of what "death on a cross" really meant. The physical torment of His death was only the smallest tip of the iceberg.

> **Deuteronomy 21:22-23** "If a man guilty of a capital offence is put to death and his body is hung on a tree, you must not leave his body on the tree overnight. Be sure to bury him that same day, because *anyone who is hung on a tree is under God's curse."*

The death that Jesus had to die was defined by the Law as the very worst of all deaths because it was a God-forsaken death. To die in such a way meant dying under the curse of His Eternal Father. For Jesus, the Eternal Son, such a loss is beyond our comprehension. Throughout His trial and beatings we never heard a word of complaint come from Jesus' lips. Yet, as He experienced the curse of the Living God against Him, He could not help but cry out, "My God, My God, why have you forsaken me?" We shudder at the depth of what was happening.

Returning to Paul's lesson, we see the extent of self-sacrifice that our life in Jesus entails. There can be no limits, no reserve. To truly have the mind of Jesus we must forsake ourselves completely. Jesus told us that to follow Him we must 'take up our cross'.

Mark 8:34-35 "Then he called the crowd to him along with his disciples and said: 'If anyone would come after me, he must deny himself and take up his cross and follow me. For whoever wants to save his life will lose it, but whoever loses his life for me and for the gospel will save it.' "

If we have understood what taking up the cross meant for Jesus, then we see what self-sacrifice it means for us too. We might want to be useful to the church family as long as it is convenient, as long as it doesn't hurt us, as long as it doesn't effect our reputation. The example of Jesus that Paul has set before us does not allow for such an attitude.

Before we get to the "second verse" of Paul's hymn, it is good for us to meditate carefully on where Paul has taken us. Let's take stock of our service and commitment to others in the church family. How are we laying down our own interests for the benefit of others? What do we possess that can be used for our local church fellowship? What can be done, however inconvenient, to help our brothers and sisters?

This lesson is meant to be learnt in "fear and trembling" (verse 12). In the next study we will see that Paul will send us out from our lesson to put it all into practice. We should be ready for that.

The hymn does have 'a second verse', and it concerns Jesus "return journey". Having given Himself up to the ultimate degree, He was then exalted to the ultimate degree.

Because Jesus did this, His Father lifted Him up, back to His glory... but Jesus returned with "a name that is above every name". Having died on the cross, Jesus is now known across the whole universe as the greatest person who ever lived. Through the Cross, His character and glory have been displayed more brightly and universally and absolutely than they could ever have been in heaven alone. The Cross has established Jesus as the rightful ruler over the whole creation, from top to bottom.

Notice in verses 6-8 that Jesus goes from heaven to earth and then even into death. In verse 10 His glory extends just as far, "in heaven and on earth and under the earth". Whether willingly or unwillingly, every single creature that has ever lived, whether angels and spirits in the heavenly realms, humans and animals on earth, or those who live under the earth, all must finally bow down before Jesus, confessing that He truly is the LORD God and be judged by Him. In the end the Name of Jesus will determine the eternal destiny of everyone.

Suffering and sacrifice first... then glory. That is the message that Peter also wanted to communicate to the church around the world in his first epistle.[20] The heart of the gospel message that the Old Testament prophets foresaw was the suffering of Jesus followed by His glory.

> **1 Peter 1:10-11** "Concerning this salvation, the prophets, who spoke of the grace that was to come to you, searched intently and with the greatest care, trying to find out the time and circumstances to which the Spirit of Christ in them was pointing when he predicted the *sufferings of Christ and the glories that would follow.*"

Because of the death and exaltation of Jesus, the pattern of 'suffering then glory' is the defining feature of the life of the church in this passing age. Jesus has set the pattern for our lives together, and as we follow Him so we are drawn together in unity and love and service. The teaching of Jesus on this is so clear and striking.

> **Luke 22:24-30** "A dispute arose among them as to which of them was considered to be greatest. Jesus said to them, 'The kings of the Gentiles lord it over them; and those who exercise authority over them call themselves Benefactors. But you are not to be like that. Instead, *the greatest among you should be like the youngest, and the one who rules like the one who serves.* For who is greater, the one who is at the table or the one who serves? Is it not the one who is at the table? But *I am among you as one who serves.* You are those who have stood by me in my trials. And I confer on you a kingdom, just as my Father conferred one on me, so that you may eat and drink at my table in my kingdom and sit on thrones, judging the twelve tribes of Israel.' "

As we share with Jesus in His trials, serving as He served, so we know that our labour is not in vain. Our future hope means that we can give away all that we have *now*, because *then* when Jesus returns we will receive everything in Him. We do not store up our treasure on earth, where it will only get taken away from us one way or another in the end. Rather, we use what we have now for the sake of the future glory that is ours in Jesus.

---

[20] See the Book by Book DVD and guide on 1 Peter.

Paul wants the Philippian church to experience the wonderful fellowship and love that happen as we stand with Jesus in the work of evangelism. Jesus utterly dedicated Himself to the work of salvation, and as we do the same so we find His blessings of love and joy more than we can imagine.

This is the pattern for our church family life together. We use all that we have, all that we are, in the service of the gospel for our brothers and sisters. Doing this shows that we are following Jesus in the way of humility and sacrifice into His future glory.

With the advance of the gospel as our purpose, with the birth, life and death of Jesus as our pattern, we reach towards the resurrection of Jesus as our future hope. *That* is how we live together as one Body, having the same mind of Jesus, loving each other with His love and being united by the Holy Spirit.

SUGGESTED QUESTIONS FOR 'YOUR ATTITUDE SHOULD BE THE SAME AS THAT OF CHRIST JESUS'. 2:1-11

1. What are the benefits of being a Christian as listed in verse1?

    How are these truths able to help the Philippian church in the suffering they are going through according to the previous verse?

2. What will make Paul's joy in relation to the Philippian church complete?

    How can the Philippian believers achieve this?

3. According to verse 3, what is the key to sharing in the unity described in verse 2?

    Why is it so difficult to adopt this attitude?

4. What is the practical day-to-day effect of considering others as better than ourselves?

5. Who should look after your interests?

    How might this attitude affect our life together as a church?

6. How are verses 5-11 connected to verses 1-4?

7. According to verses 6 and 7, what was Jesus' "very nature"?

    Why is this surprising?

8. How does the action of Jesus in verses 6-8 demonstrate the teaching of Paul in verses 3-4?

9. How is it possible to have the same attitude as Jesus had in verses 6-8? (Compare Mark 8:34-35.)

10. According to verses 9-11, what was the result of Jesus' humbling himself to such a degree?

    What is the lesson for us as we serve each other?

'Lights in the universe'

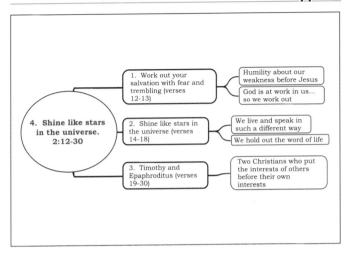

1. WORK OUT YOUR SALVATION WITH FEAR AND TREMBLING (VERSES 12-13)

"Therefore" – Paul has traced the example of Jesus from the eternal glories of heaven, down to the servant life of earth, onto the cursed death of the cross... then exalted to the highest place waiting for the total submission of the whole creation. Now it is time to bring the argument to its conclusion.

The point of the 'hymn' was to teach us how to get on with each other. Now Paul concludes that appeal.

In verse 12 he speaks to the Philippian church as his "dear friends". There is a deep fellowship between Paul and the Philippian church because of the gospel. In 1:27-28 he challenged them to live according to the gospel, and here he commends their obedience to the gospel. Note that Paul does not say that they obeyed Paul. It is the gospel of Jesus that must control them, which is what Paul always points people to. Whether he was present or absent, he knows that Jesus ultimately controlled the hearts and minds of the Philippian Christians. In fact, it is "*much more* in my absence" that they must obey, because the church must obey the apostolic gospel down the ages long after all the apostles have died.

He has just set the pattern of Jesus before them, so now he challenges them to obey that pattern in their own situation – to live it out in all they do.

Verse 12 teaches us about a proper balance, a proper understanding of our Christian living:

"work out your salvation with fear and trembling..."

"*for* it is God who works in you..."

"to will and to act..."

"according to His good purpose."

The work, the desire and the action all happen in *human* life... and yet it is our Heavenly Father who is at work according to *His* desire and purpose.

Sometimes people have spoken of this verse as a strange paradox, a logical conundrum: how can it be that both Christians and the Father are responsible for Christian living? However, Paul is not thinking of two equal causes bringing about a single effect. We work because our Father, through Jesus in the power of the Spirit, has *first* worked. We desire and act because our Father has first desired and purposed. It is not as if we are saved by the work of Jesus and are then left to do the rest of the work for ourselves. NO! After we are born again, *still* our desiring and working is all traced back to the work of the Spirit within us.

The 17th century Puritan Thomas Goodwin said that our sinful nature will only ever produce sin, but our new nature in Jesus will only ever produce goodness and righteous living. The bad tree of our sinful nature only produces bad fruit; the good tree of the new humanity in Jesus only produces good fruit. The Holy Spirit produces and gathers this good fruit from our new nature. When we find good desires within us, when we live 'worthy of the gospel', all the credit goes to the desire and purpose of the Father, who has given us new birth through Jesus and makes that new nature produce fruit by the Holy Spirit.

The phrase begins with the words "fear and trembling" (rather than "continue to work out" as in English translations). This is the first thing that Paul wants to impress upon us. The more we go on in the Christian life the more we realise that without the work of the Holy Spirit within us, our every desire, our every action, would be worthless and sinful. As we come to realise the depth and power of our sinful hearts and minds, we realise how utterly dependant we are on the constant, daily work of the Spirit. I have nothing but sin to offer... and yet, miraculously, the Spirit works to make me bear fruit by applying the finished work of Jesus to me, according to the purpose of the Father.

Paul speaks of this "fear and trembling" in other letters, and it is very useful to note how he does this.

> **1 Corinthians 2:1-5** "When I came to you, brothers, I did not come with eloquence or superior wisdom as I proclaimed to you the testimony about God. For I resolved to know nothing while I was with you except Jesus Christ and him crucified. *I came to you in weakness and fear, and with much trembling.* My message and my preaching were not with wise and persuasive words, but with a *demonstration of the Spirit's power, so that your faith might not rest on men's wisdom, but on God's power."*

Notice what caused Paul's fear and trembling. He was aware of his own weakness and dependence. He knew that he could not rely on any human ability or human wisdom because the gospel has no use for such things. Rather he was trusting only in the Spirit's power, acutely aware that he had nothing of his own to offer.

Aware of our weakness, we are aware that we are servants and not masters. Our need is for obedience and not self-confidence. We need the light of truth to guide us because we have no light of our own. We need the Word of God to instruct us, because our own words are empty.

> **2 Corinthians 7:14-16** "...our boasting about you to Titus has proved to be true as well. And his affection for you is all the greater when he remembers that you were all obedient, receiving him with *fear and trembling.* I am glad I can have complete confidence in you."

The problem with the Corinthians had been their confidence in human wisdom, but when Titus visits them he finds them filled with "fear and trembling", ready to obey the apostolic faith.

We *work out* our salvation with this fear and trembling.

This does not mean "we work to *achieve* our salvation in the terror of worrying that if we don't work hard enough we will go to Hell." *That* would be a denial of the gospel itself. No, we work out the salvation that has been given to us. We give expression to the salvation that has been freely given to us by the power of the Father, Son and Holy Spirit. Paul wants the Philippians to get on with each other, giving expression (working out) to the way of Jesus that he has just described to them.

Knowing our utter weakness, considering others better than ourselves, we nevertheless, in fear and trembling, *work*. With fear and trembling for ourselves, but with great trust and confidence in the power and purpose of the Spirit, we work out the gospel in our daily lives. When Jesus commanded the man with the withered hand to stretch it out[21], the man could have focused only on his inability to do it... and yet, in trusting the power of Jesus and forgetting his own utter inability, the man stretched out his arm.

> "The reason why we should be Christians in fear and trembling and not otherwise is that as such we put ourselves entirely into the power of God, that as such we recognise that all grace, that everything – the willing and the accomplishing, the beginning and the end, the faith and the revelation, the questions and the answers, the seeking and the finding – comes from God... Man cannot put his salvation into practice except as he recognises: it is *God!*"[22]

Notice the contrast with verse 13. We work OUT because God is at work IN. IN and OUT. We work OUT the salvation of God, because God is at work IN us. We show the gospel OUTWARDLY because it is already a reality INWARDLY.

There was a man doing a PhD in musical composition when I was at King's College. He would hunch over any piano he could find for hours, driven along by what he was doing. His explanation was this: "I have something within me that I have to get out. I must play out what is in me."

This is what Paul is telling the Christians at Philippi and therefore us too. The gospel is in us and we must get it out, express it in words and actions. We must work out, speak out, shout out, show out the gospel of Jesus Christ – because it is already at work within us.

2. SHINE LIKE STARS IN THE UNIVERSE (VERSES 14-18)

We have seen how Paul sets our gospel work as the place where the church finds its unity, and he concludes this part of his letter with a very clear expression of this.

---

[21] Matthew 12:9-13

[22] Barth, 73 and 74

As always he begins with the current problem: "do everything without complaining or arguing" (verse 14). The disunity in the Philippian church has arisen because of *grumbling* and arguing. The problem of *grumbling* might seem a small matter to us, but Paul recognises it for the severe danger that it is.

The NIV uses the word "complaining", but the word "grumbling" is better because Paul is very aware of the problem of grumbling in the ancient church under Moses.[23] We know that he is thinking of the church under Moses because in verse 15 he quotes from the Song of Moses (Deuteronomy 32:5).

When Paul wrote to the Corinthians he reminded them of the severe discipline that grumbling brought on the church in Numbers 14. He lists grumbling alongside idolatry and sexual immorality.

> **1 Corinthians 10:1-11** "For I do not want you to be ignorant of the fact, brothers, that our forefathers were all under the cloud and that they all passed through the sea. They were all baptised into Moses in the cloud and in the sea. They all ate the same spiritual food and drank the same spiritual drink; for they drank from the spiritual rock that accompanied them, and that rock was Christ. Nevertheless, God was not pleased with most of them; their bodies were scattered over the desert. *Now these things occurred as examples to keep us from setting our hearts on evil things as they did.* Do not be *idolaters*, as some of them were; as it is written: 'The people sat down to eat and drink and got up to indulge in pagan revelry.' We should not commit *sexual immorality*, as some of them did – and in one day twenty-three thousand of them died. We should not test the Lord, as some of them did – and were killed by snakes. And do not *grumble*, as some of them did – and were killed by the destroying angel. *These things happened to them as examples and were written down as warnings for us, on whom the fulfilment of the ages has come."*

Grumbling is so serious because it is the fruit of ingratitude and selfishness. Grumbling indicates that we are not satisfied with the LORD Jesus. In Exodus 16 and Numbers 14, the people grumbled against Moses and Aaron. They complained that things were too hard, that the miraculous food was boring, that life in the desert with pagan enemies was too difficult. Instead of

---

23 *'Murmurings'.* The word is constantly used in the LXX (Greek translation of the Hebrew Scriptures) of Israel in the wilderness." Lightfoot, 117

BookbyBook

being satisfied with Christ who accompanied them, they had set their hearts on selfish interests. Instead of trusting Him to care for them they grumbled. This grumbling caused the church in the wilderness to be divided.

> Be ye not like Israel of old. Never give way to discontent and murmuring, to questioning and unbelief. [24]

Grumbling and arguing always go together. All that Paul has taught since 2:1 has been focused on dealing with this problem. There can be no grumbling and therefore no arguing if the church family follows the way of Jesus, who had plenty of reasons to grumble if we consider verses 6-8. Jesus never grumbled because He trusted His Father and kept His heart fixed on what His Father sent Him to do.

In this way Paul reminds the Philippians of what the purpose of their life is – "to shine like stars in the universe as you hold out the word of life."

Verse 15 is a call to faithful gospel witness in a world that so desperately needs it. If we grumble and argue, setting our hearts on comfort and self-interest, then we are just the same as the perishing world around us. We are no good to anybody. We may still talk about the gospel, but what impact can it have if we do not even believe it in practice ourselves!

The alternative to verse 14 is being "blameless and pure". These words describe what is unmixed or unadulterated. If grumbling and arguing occur when worldly desires and unbelief are allowed into our hearts, then the remedy is for us to be 100% focused on the gospel of Jesus.

The contrast is with those who betray the gospel of Jesus – "a crooked and depraved generation". This phrase is taken from the Song of Moses in Deuteronomy 32:5:

> **Deuteronomy 32:4-6** "A faithful God who does no wrong, upright and just is He. They have acted corruptly towards him; to their shame they are no longer his children, but a warped and crooked generation. Is this the way you repay the LORD, O foolish and unwise people? Is he not your Father, your Creator, who made you and formed you?"

---

[24] Lightfoot, 116

Notice that Moses is not speaking about the world in general, but about Israel in particular. The LORD formed Israel as His children, and yet they do not believe in Him. He is "upright and just", yet they act corruptly. In Acts 2:40, Peter uses the same phrase to refer to the unbelieving people of God in Jerusalem.

So, Paul seems to be calling on the Philippians to reject the compromise and unbelief and false teaching that so many in the churches had fallen into, and instead throw themselves into the work of evangelism and loving service. They are to "shine like stars" in the cosmos, offering the word of life (verse 16).

We look up at the night sky and in the darkness we see the lights shining. We are reminded of John 1:5 – Jesus is the light of the world, but "the Light shines in the darkness, but the darkness has not understood it." As the people of Jesus, we too shine His light in the darkness of unbelief and ignorance.[25] Those in the churches who follow a false gospel or their own evil desires are "a crooked and depraved generation", because the only remedy for the darkness of the world is the pure gospel of Jesus. It is desperately important that with fear and trembling we work out this salvation and faithfully offer it to a dark and dying world.

The only activity that lasts into eternity is our gospel witness. This is what bears spiritual fruit. Nothing else that we do will last beyond this passing age. All our selfish interests perish with us, but the fruit of the gospel lasts forever. So, verse 16, Paul knows that if the Philippians purely and unitedly offer the gospel to the world, then there will be real fruit to show on the Day of Christ. Paul is anxious that all the work that he has put into the Philippian church will come to nothing if they become a "crooked and depraved generation" by wasting their lives in arguments.

However, (verses 17-18) Paul has confidence about the Philippian church. Rather than pouring his life away for no return, he sees the Philippian church as a wonderful sacrifice that pleases the LORD God. He sees himself as the drink offering poured out on top of that sacrifice – so that Paul and the Philippians can rejoice together in their efforts.

---

[25] The fact that Paul uses the word 'cosmos' here reminds us of the huge canvas that the gospel of Jesus is painted on. Ephesians 3:10-11 tells us that the Father's "intent was that now, through the church, the manifold wisdom of God should be made known to the rulers and authorities in the heavenly realms, according to his eternal purpose which he accomplished in Christ Jesus our Lord." Our gospel witness is watched by more than the world of humanity.

In the Hebrew Scriptures the drink offering signified a life dedicated in service to the LORD God. A drink offering involved pouring out wine, either on its own or more usually over an animal sacrifice. The Scriptures frequently connect wine and blood (for example, see Genesis 49:11; John 2:3-4; Luke 22:20; 1 Cor. 11:25-27). Leviticus 17:11-14 tells us that the life of a creature is in its blood. So, we find that a drink offering is used to indicate a life dedicated to the Lord's service.[26]

The Philippian church's gospel work was a sacrifice pleasing to the LORD... and Paul rejoiced with them in that his effort was the drink offering sharing in that sacrifice.

3. TIMOTHY AND EPAPHRODITUS (VERSES 19-30)

All of Paul's plans and hopes are *"in the Lord Jesus"* (verse 19). In many ways that is the crucial phrase that we must grasp in these verses. Notice the repetition of the phrase in verses 24 and 29. Paul's great complaint is that everyone looks out for their own interests. They plan and decide based on their own analysis and desires. In all these verses before us we must realise that for Paul *everything* is "in Jesus". Even though Paul's plans are all part of his apostolic work, yet he takes no authority on himself for the future. The future belongs to Jesus, and the life of Paul, Timothy and the Philippian church are all united in Jesus, under His divine care and authority.

The Christian is a part of Christ, a member of His body. His every thought and word and deed proceeds from Christ, as the centre of volition. Thus he loves in the Lord, he hopes in the Lord, he boasts in the Lord, he labours in the Lord, etc. He has one guiding principle in acting and in forbearing to act – *only to the Lord* (1 Cor. 7:39)[27]

Paul's attitude is just what James describes:

---

[26] We first encounter the drink offering in Genesis 35:14. Genesis 34 records the wicked and shameful behaviour of the church in the Promised Land, and in Genesis 35 Jacob returns to Bethel, where the LORD had appeared to him. In Gen 35:2 Jacob purifies his household from compromise and idolatry. In Gen 35:9-13 the covenant is renewed to Jacob and he responds by setting up a pillar over which he pours wine and oil. The drink offering indicates his life being poured out in service for the LORD and the oil indicates the necessity of the Spirit for such a life. Thus, in the Law of Moses we see that the morning and evening sacrifices were to be accompanied with a drink offering (see Numbers 28 & 29). The animal is given as an atoning sacrifice, but the proper response to that is the Israelites' life poured out in service to the Father, Son and Holy Spirit.

[27] Lightfoot, 120

> **James 4:13-15** "Now listen, you who say, 'Today or tomorrow we will go to this or that city, spend a year there, carry on business and make money.' Why, you do not even know what will happen tomorrow. What is your life? You are a mist that appears for a little while and then vanishes. Instead, you ought to say, 'If it is the Lord's will, we will live and do this or that.'"

Paul hopes *in the Lord Jesus* to send Timothy to the Philippians. It is clear that they have been very anxious about Paul, but he is also anxious about them. He knows that they are suffering persecution (1:30), so he wants to find out exactly how they are doing.

In verses 20-22 Paul praises Timothy, who is so unlike all the other church leaders. Only Timothy genuinely cares for the Philippians (verse 20). Perhaps few others had visited the Philippian church or knew anything about them. Others might express an interest, pray the odd prayer for them or politely listen to all that Paul has to say, but only Timothy really cares for them. In verse 21 we are looking back to verse 4. *Then* Paul asked us to care for the interests of "others" rather than our own. Now he takes us to the real issue that lay behind even verse 4.

The fundamental issue of life itself is whether we care for our own interests or the interests of *Jesus Christ*.

If we care as Jesus cares then, of course, we will put the interests of the church family above our own. Paul's hopes (verse 19) were "in the Lord Jesus" and now we understand more of what that mighty and deep phrase means. Paul's hopes are set according to the interests of Jesus.

Paul's verdict is very bleak. *Everyone* "looks out for his own interests, not those of Jesus Christ." Paul only knows of faithful companion Timothy who cares more for Jesus than his own interests. If we think Paul is being too harsh or merely rhetorical, we must remember that even this beloved Philippian church have just been diagnosed as suffering this same disease (2:3-4). Every time I read verse 21, I flinch knowing how firmly I would have fallen under Paul's condemnation. If only one of Paul's companions genuinely loved Jesus as they should, then none of us can ever be complacent. How would each of us have fared if Paul had asked us about our love of Jesus and humanity?

However, the Philippians had met Timothy, so Paul was confident that they would agree with his verdict (verse 22). Timothy had been like a son to Paul...

and he had taken after his 'father'. Paul and Timothy had worked side by side for Jesus in their gospel work. Timothy had seen and imitated the way Paul placed every aspect of his life "in the Lord Jesus."

Once Paul knew how things were going to work out for him, in terms of his trial and imprisonment, then he would be able to send Timothy to the Philippians (verse 23). Verse 24 again shows us the mind of Paul. He had analysed how the interests of Jesus could best be served, in terms of his own life and death (1:20-26), so he now expresses his confidence "*in the Lord*" that he too will be able to visit the Philippian church.

Paul wanted the Philippian church to have some immediate help, though. So, he was going to send Epaphroditus to them. He too was an excellent example of a servant of Jesus.

Paul gives four titles to Epaphroditus – his brother; fellow-worker; fellow-soldier; "your messenger" (verse 25). He is Paul's brother because he is a Christian just like Paul. The gospel brings us into the wonderful, diverse, international, united family of Jesus Christ. He is a fellow-worker with Paul, advancing the gospel and building up the church. He is also a fellow-soldier, fighting for the gospel against false-teaching and worthless living. Finally, he is a messenger, sent by the Philippian church specifically to look after Paul. This is yet another proof of their great love for Paul. He, like Paul and Timothy, has great concern for his home church (verse 26). He knows how worried his church family will be because they had heard how ill he was.

Why was Epaphroditus so ill? Verse 30 gives us the clue – "he almost died for the work of Christ, risking his life to make up for the help you could not give me." He had been sent to help Paul. Paul's dedication was absolute and his work-load massive.

> **2 Corinthians 6:4-5** "as servants of God we commend ourselves in every way: in great endurance; in troubles, hardships and distresses; in beatings, imprisonments and riots; in hard work, sleepless nights and hunger..."

Epaphroditus gambled his own life and health in his desire to help Paul in the work of Christ. Hard work and sleepless nights, missing meals and facing danger – in all these ways and more, Epaphroditus faced one of the very common hazards of Christian ministry. He became so over-worked and exhausted that he fell seriously ill and he nearly died (verse 27). [28]

Paul had clearly come to love the company of Epaphroditus and would have been very deeply upset to lose him. The Father had mercy and healed Epaphroditus (verse 27). There is a very sweet note in verse 28. He wants to send Epaphroditus back to the Philippians so that they wouldn't worry about him, but also so that Paul himself "may have less anxiety." Clearly, as much as Paul loved this earnest brother, he knew that Epaphroditus would not be able to cope with the pace of Paul's apostolic labour. Paul didn't want Epaphroditus ill again, so he sent him back to the regular difficulties and hard work of Philippi.

However, verse 29, even though Epaphroditus had become wounded in the gospel work, he was to be honoured, [29] along with any others that suffered in the same way. We need to take this seriously today. Many churches have people who have burned out in gospel work and Bible teaching. Sometimes such people simply need time to rest and time to develop a more manageable work pattern. Sometimes this can take a long time or maybe they will never be able to work as they once did. It is very important that the church family is very patient and supportive of such Christian workers. They have risked their lives, their health and comfort, for the sake of Jesus, even if they have no visible wounds to show for it.

Timothy and Epaphroditus challenge us. Timothy's great love for the Philippians and his dedication to evangelism shows us the model of a church minister that Paul had in mind. Epaphroditus was so full of zeal that he almost killed himself working for Jesus. Epaphroditus did not seem to have a single thought for his own interests... so Paul had to look out for him by sending him back to Philippi.

Both men challenge us because both of them put the interests of Jesus and the church family ahead of their own.

---

[28] One of the most helpful books on dealing with this aspect of Christian work is by Marjory Foyle, *"Honourably Wounded"*, Kregel 2001

[29] Hence the title of Marjory's excellent book.

SUGGESTED QUESTIONS FOR 'SHINE LIKE STARS IN THE UNIVERSE. 2:12-30

1. What does "therefore" signify in verse 12?

    How can the humility, service, obedience and glory of Jesus make a difference to the way we live today?

2. Why does Paul describe working out our salvation as involving "fear and trembling " in verse 12? (Compare 1 Corinthians 2:1-5.)

3. Why might there be a tendency to complain or grumble if we are living the life that Jesus has demonstrated for us?

4. How can you shine like a star (verse 15) in the situation you are in at home or at school or at work?

5. How might the life of a Christian be wasted in light of eternity?

6. What is the controlling influence on all Paul's actions and plans for the future?

7. How does Timothy's life reflect the teaching of 2:1-4?

8. What four titles does Paul use to describe Epaphroditus? What does this tell us about the sort of person he was?

5. The power of His resurrection and the fellowship of sharing in His sufferings. 3:1-21

'Citizens of heaven'

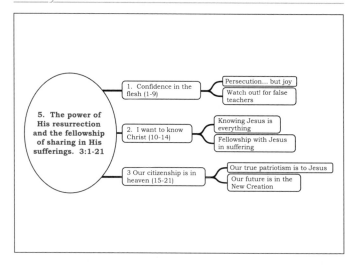

1. Confidence in the flesh (1-9) → Persecution... but joy / Watch out! for false teachers

5. The power of His resurrection and the fellowship of sharing in His sufferings. 3:1-21

2. I want to know Christ (10-14) → Knowing Jesus is everything / Fellowship with Jesus in suffering

3 Our citizenship is in heaven (15-21) → Our true patriotism is to Jesus / Our future is in the New Creation

1. CONFIDENCE IN THE FLESH (1-9)

Chapter 3 shows us the secondary problem that was facing the Philippian church. The main problem, as at Corinth, was division – as it so often is in and between our churches today. Paul has shown that the solution to that problem is to be focused on the gospel work of salvation, just as Jesus Himself was. He set aside His own interests for the sake of the gospel... and if we all do the same then we will be united with a common mind, mutual love and the same purpose.

If that is the great solution to the churches' problems (and the great answer to the world's crisis facing the anger of the Living God), then the greatest danger to *that* is a *false* gospel: a way of thinking, a message that is not the true good news about Jesus.

In chapter 1 Paul told the Philippians to contend for the faith of the gospel without being afraid of any opponents, and now he is about to unmask some very dangerous opponents. However, before he begins his solemn and passionate warning, he again recommends joy in the Lord.

Our life in Jesus is a life of constant opposition and effort in this passing age. It is what Jesus promised to us. Yet in promising opposition to us, He also promised that we will know His joy and in the end, at the end of this age, we will triumph with Him.

> **Luke 21:17-19** "All men will hate you because of me. But not a hair of your head will perish. By standing firm *you will gain life*."

> **Matthew 10:22-23** "All men will hate you because of me, but *he who stands firm to the end will be saved*. When you are persecuted in one place, flee to another."

> **John 16:33** "I have told you these things, so that in me you may have peace. In this world you will have trouble. *But take heart! I have overcome the world.*"

> **Luke 6:22-23** "Blessed are you when men hate you, when they exclude you and insult you and reject your name as evil, because of the Son of Man. *Rejoice in that day and leap for joy*, because great is your reward in heaven. For that is how their fathers treated the prophets."

Jesus tells us not to be down-hearted or disillusioned when we experience opposition and conflict for Him. Rather, we are to take this as a sign that we stand in the line of the faithful prophets. We should leap for joy, because we are so closely identified with Jesus and our future hope will become more and more certain to us. Joy is always present in the authentic Christian life, never more so than when we are standing together holding out the true gospel to a dying world.

So, before Paul deals with the problem of opposition in the Philippian church he reminds the saints to rejoice in the Lord. The fact that our joy is "in the Lord" means that it does not depend on the varying circumstances of this world. In Him we find true, lasting joy that cannot be taken away from us.

Paul returns to the age-old problem of false teaching in the church. Since the beginning of the world the church has been constantly threatened by such false teaching (see Jude 11-16). Although Paul has warned of this earlier in this letter, yet he is not weary of sounding this warning because it ensures the safety of the Philippian Christians (verse 1). [30]

In verse 2, the original Greek is much stronger than the NIV translation: Paul says "*Watch out* for those dogs! *Watch out* for those evil doers! *Watch out* for

---

[30] It is possible that Paul has written earlier letters to the Philippians. In Polycarp's letter to the Philippians we see a possible reference to other letters that Paul wrote to them. However, it might be the case that Polycarp said *that* precisely because of this verse!

those mutilators!" It is a strong and urgent warning, and it is good that we first grasped our joy in the Lord.

As we survey these verses we can quickly see the nature of the problem. Such is the strength of Paul's language that we need to spend a moment getting the full background. Paul is not speaking about a local issue affecting only the Philippians. He is warning of a terrible danger that was attacking the whole people of God across the world, Jew and Gentile alike.

> **Note:** Remember that Paul was a *Jewish* believer in Jesus. He didn't cease to be Jewish when he followed Jesus. Quite the opposite. Jesus is the *Jewish* Messiah and a Jew who follows Jesus is not denying but completing or fulfilling their Jewishness. [31] It is vital that we understand that Paul is contending *for* the *Jewish* Messiah and *for* Jewish identity, not being anti-Semitic in any way.

One of the great issues of the day was the true meaning of the Hebrew Scriptures and the Law of Moses in particular. Not all the Jews trusted in the Jewish Messiah, the One spoken of by Moses and the prophets (John 1:45). Some rejected Him completely so that they could continue to trust merely in the Law itself, giving them room for boasting and religious pride. Others found a place for Jesus alongside the Law, as a kind of supplement.

At the beginning of Acts 15 the false teaching is spelled out very clearly for us:

> **Acts 15:1-2** "Some men came down from Judea to Antioch and were teaching the brothers: 'Unless you are circumcised, according to the custom taught by Moses, you cannot be saved.' This brought Paul and Barnabas into sharp dispute and debate with them. So Paul and Barnabas were appointed, along with some other believers, to go up to Jerusalem to see the apostles and elders about this question."

Paul, and all the church leaders (at the Council of Jerusalem [32]) recognised the terrible danger of these renegade Jews. These unbelieving Jews had rejected the entire message of the Hebrew Scriptures, but were determined to

---

[31] "Paul did not teach that Christ obliterates the distinctives of Jewishness any more than He obliterates the distinctives of male or femaleness. But our core identity is that we are part of His body, one with all believers of all times and places. 'Therefore, if anyone is in Messiah, he is a new creation; the old has gone, the new has come!' (2 Corinthians 5:17)." (The Challenge Of Our Messianic Movement, Part 2: Us and Him by Rich Robinson and Ruth Rosen, on the Jews for Jesus website: www.jewsforjesus.org)

[32] See Acts 15:3-33

infiltrate and undermine the global expansion of Israel. As the Gentile believers were being grafted into Israel, some of the 'natural' members of Israel were trying to control the way in which Gentiles joined. They were trying to deflect the people of God from trusting only in the Messiah.

When we look through Paul's letters we see how these unbelieving Jews were troubling congregations across the world, insisting that unless a person was circumcised they could not be part of Israel.

1 Corinthians 7:19 "*Circumcision is nothing and uncircumcision is nothing.* Keeping God's commands is what counts."

Listen to these incredibly stirring words from Paul's manifesto of freedom, his letter to the Galatians.

Galatians 5:1-7 "It is for freedom that Christ has set us free. Stand firm, then, and do not let yourselves be burdened again by a yoke of slavery. Mark my words! I, Paul, tell you that *if you let yourselves be circumcised, Christ will be of no value to you at all*. Again I declare to every man who lets himself be circumcised that he is required to obey the whole law. You who are trying to be justified by law have been alienated from Christ; you have fallen away from grace. But by faith we eagerly await through the Spirit the righteousness for which we hope. For *in Christ Jesus neither circumcision nor uncircumcision has any value. The only thing that counts is faith expressing itself through love.* You were running a good race. Who cut in on you and kept you from obeying the truth?"

Paul reassured the Ephesian church that they were now a full part of Israel, without ever being circumcised in the flesh. Although naturally foreigners to Israel, they had been included in 'citizenship in Israel' through the blood of Christ:

Ephesians 2:11-13 "...remember that formerly you who are Gentiles by birth and called 'uncircumcised' by *those who call themselves 'the circumcision'* (that done in the body by the hands of men) – remember that at that time you were separate from Christ, excluded from citizenship in Israel and foreigners to the covenants of the promise, without hope and without God in the world. But now in Christ Jesus you who once were far away have been brought near through the blood of Christ."

The Colossians too are told that they have the reality of circumcision without ever having the outward bodily sign.

> **Colossians 2:11** "In him *you were also circumcised, in the putting off of the sinful nature, not with a circumcision done by the hands of men but with the circumcision done by Christ…*"

Finally, when Paul wrote to Titus he had to warn him about these people who trusted in the Law and its commands rather than the Messiah that the Law was describing.

> **Titus 1:10-11** "…there are many rebellious people, mere talkers and deceivers, especially those of the circumcision group. They must be silenced, because they are ruining whole households by teaching things they ought not to teach…"

So, as we study this chapter we need to keep the big picture in mind. The issue of legal righteousness versus the righteousness of Jesus will not face us all in quite that form today [33], but the principle remains the same (as we will see).

Notice how Paul begins Philippians chapter 3. He describes the false teachers as *"dogs"* and "mutilators of the flesh".[34] On the other hand he describes the Philippian church as *"the circumcision"*.

This is a very sharp introduction. The dog is an unclean animal according to the Law (see Leviticus 11, particularly verse 27). In Matthew 15 we see that 'dogs' were a way of referring to the unclean Gentiles.[35] On the other hand the Philippians were Gentiles who trusted in Jesus the Messiah.

---

[33] Not all Christians face the people that believe that they need to be circumcised or follow the Law of Moses in order to be saved. There are such groups around and we need to reject them very firmly. However, for must of us the threat comes in the more subtle form of asking us to take pride in anything of the flesh.

[34] There is a play on words here. Paul uses the word *"katatome"* (mutilation) and then the word *"peritome"* (circumcision).

[35] Matthew 15:22-28 "A *Canaanite* woman from that vicinity came to him, crying out, 'Lord, Son of David, have mercy on me! My daughter is suffering terribly from demon-possession.' Jesus did not answer a word. So his disciples came to him and urged him, 'Send her away, for she keeps crying out after us.' He answered, 'I was sent only to the lost sheep of Israel.' The woman came and knelt before him. 'Lord, help me!' she said. He replied, 'It is not right to take the children's bread and toss it to their *dogs*.' 'Yes, Lord,' she said, 'but even the *dogs* eat the crumbs that fall from their masters' table.' Then Jesus answered, 'Woman, you have great faith! Your request is granted.'"

Paul turns the world of "the circumcision" group upside down when he calls the unbelieving Jews "dogs" whose precious circumcision was a mere mutilation of the flesh. He also refers to the uncircumcised Gentile Philippians as "the circumcision", going back to the point that we saw in his other letters: *true circumcision is not a matter of what we do to our bodies but whether we trust only in Jesus or not.*

In Leviticus 29:27 and 21:5 we see that mere cutting of the body was a pagan practice. See especially 1 Kings 18:28, when the priests of Baal mutilate their bodies as they try to get Baal's attention. Paul is showing that those Jews who reject Jesus are mere pagans who worship a false god! There is no hesitation about Paul's language!

Verse 3 gets to the heart of the whole matter. Paul and the Philippians, whether outwardly circumcised or not, whether Jew or Gentile, are the LORD God's people, possessing the reality of circumcision (through new birth) and offering true worship in the Spirit, enjoying the glory of the Messiah, Jesus.

> "We possess the true circumcision not of the flesh but of the heart, and we also offer the true worship, the service not of external rites but of spiritual worship." [36]

The end of verse 3 is crucial, because it shows us that although the specific heresy of trusting in circumcision is not so common today, yet the real issue is putting "confidence in the flesh". Any practice or teaching that causes us to put any confidence in the flesh, in the merely external (the 'religious'), drags us into exactly the same danger that Paul speaks of here.

From verse 4, Paul tackles the possibility of putting confidence in the flesh. The false teachers thought that the Law of Moses provides lots of ways of achieving 'credit' in the eyes of the Living God. They believed that it was possible to be more or less favoured by the LORD God depending on outward factors.

So, Paul faces them on their own ground. He had all the "righteous" qualifications that they trusted in, yet he had seen through them all. If we notice all the things that Paul lists we get an insight into the mentality of the false teachers.

[36] Lightfoot, 145

1. Circumcised on the eighth day.	He was not a late convert to Judaism. He was circumcised as a baby on the eighth day, just as it was written in Genesis 17:12
2. An Israelite.	Not a Gentile.
3. Of the tribe of Benjamin.	The tribe of Benjamin had been a faithful tribe and the first king, Saul (after whom Paul had been named), was from the tribe of Benjamin.
4. Hebrew parents.	A Hebrew born from Hebrew parents. Neither of his parents were Gentiles.
5. A Pharisee.	A member of the most zealous group of those who trusted in the Law.
6. Had persecuted the church.	Paul had been prepared to kill people in his zeal for the Law.
7. Legally faultless.	From an outward, fleshly point of view, Paul had been scrupulous in obeying the Law.

The false teachers would have dreamt of having a CV like Paul's. He had all the right qualifications and had gone to the "right school". Surely, they would think, anyone with such a "righteous" pedigree would be able to hold his head up high in the presence of the LORD God of Israel!

Paul has some serious news – verse 7. When Paul carefully assesses the genuine, spiritual value of all those outward marks of "righteousness" he regards them not as *profit* but loss for the sake of the Jewish Messiah. The "circumcision" people would have viewed all the things Paul listed as spiritual profit, qualities that gave a person credit in the nation of Israel. Paul says that when a person knows the Messiah, they realise that all those things go in the account book in the *loss* column. They are less than worthless.

Paul goes further (verse 8). He considers *"everything"* a *loss* compared to the infinite *profit* of knowing Jesus – "Christ Jesus *my Lord.*"

Everything that Paul ever took pride in, all has been rejected, because Jesus is so infinitely more valuable.

Paul's language here becomes very strong and most English translations are very delicate. The NIV puts "I consider them *rubbish* that I may gain Christ…" The old King James version more accurately notes that Paul has to "count them but *dung*, that I may win Christ…" Paul could not be more offensive to those who trust in the flesh. He says that all their precious religion, all their Law-trusting, all their outward zeal is not just loss, but belongs down the toilet. This is Paul at his most passionate and blunt.

As long as a person continues to trust in *anything* other than Christ they have not laid hold of Jesus. As long as they think that anything else can help them be righteous before the Living God they have not yet grasped Jesus the Messiah. He will save only those who abandon every other hope. That is why Paul says in verse 9 that he wants simply to be "found" in Christ, not having anything of his own to offer at all. He doesn't want anything that comes from trusting in the Law, but only the righteousness that is freely given as a person trusts their life, death and eternity to Jesus. *That* is the only righteousness that has any validity before the LORD God, because it is the only righteousness that is *given* by the LORD God. Notice how Paul *twice* in verse 9 describes this righteousness as coming "by faith".

Can we see the power of Paul's argument? Paul is terrified that false teachers would come into the churches and suggest to them that they need some other kind of "righteousness" alongside the freely given *divine* righteousness of Jesus. In our situation today, there might be all kinds of religious practices or traditions that have this same effect. If there is anything that makes us feel more acceptable to God other then Jesus, then it must be rejected as strongly as we possibly can. It is complete sewage that will make us unclean before a Holy God. If Paul speaks so strongly about this we dare not be casual about it.

It might be good to pray about this right now. Ask the Holy Spirit to open your eyes to any false confidence so that you can trust in Jesus alone with only His righteousness.

All I once held dear, built my life upon,
All this world reveres and wars to own;
All I once thought gain I have counted loss,
Spent and worthless now compared to this.

Knowing You, Jesus, knowing You
There is no greater thing.
You're my all, You're the best,
You're my joy, my righteousness,
And I love you Lord.

Now my heart's desire is to know You more,
To be found in You and known as Yours
To possess by faith what I could not earn
All surpassing gift of righteousness

Oh to know the power of Your risen life,
And to know You in Your sufferings;
To become like You in Your death, my Lord,
So with You to live and never die. [37]

2. I WANT TO KNOW CHRIST (10-14)

Given the "spiritual maths" that Paul has been doing, we see clearly that there is only one thing that has any real value – "knowing Jesus."

We all need to take this spiritual check-up regularly. It is so easy to get taken up with the "things" of the Christian faith – the duties, the discussions, the activities, the questions. As important as any of these "things" might ever be, they must only ever be side-shows to the main event – knowing Jesus.

The moment that we are not utterly thrilled by Jesus, we know that we have become spiritually sick and we need desperate spiritual healing.

I have noticed that some people speak only of 'God'. I assume they are referring to our Heavenly Father, but sometimes they use the word 'God' so much and the word 'Jesus' so little that I just begin to wonder what place Jesus *really* has in their heart and mind.

The apostle Paul never got tired of talking and writing about Jesus. When he wrote about the love of the Father, he wrote about the sending of Jesus. When he wrote about the ultimate purposes of the Father, he wrote about the second coming and triumph of Jesus. When he wrote about the righteousness of God, he wrote about trusting in Jesus. Let's examine ourselves to see the place that Jesus *really* has in us... not what we *think* that He has.

---

[37] Graham Kendrick, ©1993 Make Way Music

But, Paul does not "know Jesus" in some undefined or abstract way. We know Jesus in and through His Cross and Resurrection (verse 10). Jesus is not available to us in any other way. To know Jesus is to be joined to Him in His death and resurrection.[38] If we want to know the glorious, ascended Jesus who sits at the right hand of the Father in heaven, then we first meet Him at the Cross.

However, Paul is not simply talking about believing the right things about Jesus. Paul wants to *experience* the *power* of Jesus' resurrection and "*the fellowship of sharing* in His sufferings, *becoming like Him* in His death…" All this is experiential language.

He wants to know Jesus as he walks the *way of Jesus*.

The power of the resurrection gives us new birth and gives us the certain hope of our glorious new creation future with Jesus. But this has another effect. In being united to Jesus by new birth, we are no longer part of *this* world, this *passing* age. Therefore, we find ourselves dead to *this* world and hated by it. The words of Jesus in John 15 are so powerful:

> **John 15:18-21** "If the world hates you, keep in mind that it hated me first. If you belonged to the world, it would love you as its own. As it is, *you do not belong to the world, but I have chosen you out of the world. That is why the world hates you*. Remember the words I spoke to you: 'No servant is greater than his master.' If they persecuted me, they will persecute you also. If they obeyed my teaching, they will obey yours also. They will treat you this way because of my name, for they do not know the One who sent me."

The power of the resurrection lifts us from death to life… but this is precisely what causes us to be hated by the world. The power of the resurrection brings with it the hatred and persecution of the world. YET, in being hated by the world, in treating as dung all that the flesh values, we are in deep fellowship with Jesus. That is the path that He walked and as we walk it too we find ourselves close to Him. Knowing His fellowship as we experience something of what He experienced is a great joy even in the deepest pain.

In walking with Jesus in suffering we know that we are heading towards the great and final resurrection. Jesus was resurrected after His suffering, so we are certain that in walking with Him we will eventually end up with the same

---

[38] See Romans 6:5

resurrection (verse 11). We hear the wonder in Paul as he contemplates that the same resurrection that happened to Jesus will also happen to him.

Notice the progression of what Paul says. From the power of the resurrection, through suffering and death, ending up with the resurrection. The power of the resurrection gives us spiritual life and starts us on the way of the Cross with Jesus. We walk with Him in all that we must suffer until we die. Then we look forward to our bodily resurrection at the end when Jesus returns.

Verses 12-14 stand in parallel to verses 7-9. "A righteousness of my own" is equivalent to "I have already obtained all this". The foolishness that thinks that it can boast through the Law is the same foolishness that thinks it can claim the resurrection as a reward. It is quite possible that the false teachers taught that 'perfection' was available for those who worked hard enough.

The proper attitude before Jesus is one of total humility and dependance. I can achieve nothing no matter how hard I run, because in myself I have no power, no goodness, no faith.

First, always *first,* Jesus takes hold of us... and then, in His strength and by His permission, we take hold of Him (verse 12).

Those that work hard to perfect themselves put their confidence in their flesh. They believe that they possess the zeal and the power (perhaps with a little help...) to apprehend the goal of perfection. But, the one who trusts Jesus presses on, works hard, runs with all their strength, not because they can obtain the prize for themselves, but because *the LORD Jesus* calls us (and draws us) to the finish line to give us the prize freely (verse 14).

Our perfection and our bodily redemption lie in the hands of Jesus for the future, not in our hands.

> "Seeing that He has made Himself known to me as Lord, that His righteousness never again lets go of me in faith, that the power of His resurrection has placed me in the fellowship of His sufferings. Seeing that this is so... I run and am well content to be only a runner, content not to have apprehended, content to stretch out empty hands. To be apprehended is enough.[39] "

---

[39] Barth, 108

3   OUR CITIZENSHIP IS IN HEAVEN (15-21)

Throughout this section of the letter the apostle Paul is full of literary skill and passion. In verse 12 Paul said that he had not already been "made perfect", but he begins verse 15 by saying "all of us who *are perfect*..." Well, is he perfect or not?!

It seems that Paul is using the language that the false teachers were using in order to reach the Philippians. Perhaps they claimed to be perfect.

If they really are 'perfect' then they will understand all that Paul has just explained and agree with him. If they think differently, but are genuinely seeking spiritual maturity, then the Holy Spirit will guide them into the truth.

> "*Teleioi* (perfect) is obviously a slogan or catch-word, perhaps the very one used by the opposition party with their eagerness for Christians to perform special actions and be in a special moral and ritual state. [40]"

Real Christian maturity is shown when Christians are deeply aware of their own weakness and dependence. The genuinely 'perfect' are those who run with empty hands towards Jesus who has everything in His hands.

Instead of reaching for the illusionary 'perfection' of the 'dogs', the Philippians should build on what they *really do* have. When they began to follow Jesus they knew that they had nothing, that they could do nothing. That is what they need to keep on living (verse 16).

> "...the apostle is confident that a desire to know the truth in full measure will be rewarded by God's revelation (verse 15). In the meanwhile, he goes on, until you do see things like this, be open-minded and teachable, and guide your life by what you know to be true. [41]"

The Philippians had seen what a mature Christian was like when Paul was with them. They should imitate Paul. Why? Because, as he says in 1 Corinthians 11:1 "Imitate me as I imitate Christ."

---

[40] Barth, 111

[41] Ralph Martin, *The New Century Bible Commentary*, Eerdmans, Grand Rapids, 1989, 141

Paul has no interests of his own, only the interests of Jesus.

If we want to see what a justified sinner looks like… a sinner who has given themselves over to Jesus, then Paul is the example that the Scriptures set before us. When people speak about perfection or act in a triumphant way over their weakness, Paul is our model. He 'boasts' about his weaknesses and does not hide the fact that he still struggles with his sin all the time (see Romans 7).

> **2 Corinthians 11:29-30** "Who is weak, and I do not feel weak? Who is led into sin, and I do not inwardly burn? If I must boast, I will boast of the things that show my weakness."

Throughout this chapter Paul has pleaded with the Philippians (and us) to live according to the gospel. The moment we put any confidence in the flesh we have rejected Jesus, whether that be through keeping the Law or through some kind of 'perfectionist' mentality that makes us think that we have already 'arrived'. Paul and the apostles have shown us the pattern of life that the gospel demands… and *that* is why the New Testament tells us so much about the life and struggles of the apostles and their friends.

In verses 18-19 Paul pronounces a very solemn verdict – so many of these so-called "Christians" live as if they were enemies. This made Paul weep. The false teachers he condemns with harsh words, but the victims of their teaching produce such great sadness in this most loving apostle. For all their zeal they have been led onto a path that leads only to hell. They might have an outward show of great religious zeal and moral purity – and yet underneath it all they are earthly minded and worldly. They show by their lives that they are doomed to destruction, that they worship their own bodies, that they set their hearts on merely earthly things.

Some have argued that the opponents of verses 18-19 are a different group than the earlier part of chapter 3. It is certainly possible, but I'm not sure. One of the remarkable truths that I have learnt time after time is that human religion, no matter how morally zealous and pious it tries to be, no matter how solemnly it holds its scriptures, offers no defence at all against the sinfulness of the human heart. In fact, in trying to cover up our sinful corruption, we are in a worse state. Some of the worst examples of worldliness and selfishness go on under the cover of legalism and religion.

Colossians 2:21-23 "'Do not handle! Do not taste! Do not touch!'? These are all destined to perish with use, because they are based on human commands and teachings. *Such regulations indeed have an appearance of wisdom, with their self-imposed worship, their false humility and their harsh treatment of the body, but they lack any value in restraining sensual indulgence.*"

My own personal view is that verses 18-19 are still concerned with the same Law-trusting parasites as the earlier part of the chapter.

Notice that their loose living makes them enemies of the *Cross of Christ*. Some opponents of Jesus, down the centuries, have argued that the gospel of free forgiveness through Jesus' death will simply lead to moral licence – that is, if a person thinks that the the Cross will freely take away all their sins, then they may as well sin all the time. However, here Paul shows us that the very opposite is the case. Those that fix their hearts and minds on merely earthly things find no comfort in the Cross of Christ. They are enemies of the Cross. The Cross of Jesus is what unmasks all selfish, earthly living. We have already seen in this letter that the way of Jesus to the Cross destroys all selfish desires, all self-serving agendas. Anyone who tries to excuse worldliness by looking to the free grace of Jesus' death will find no comfort whatsoever.

When Paul says (verse 19) that "their god is their stomach", he could be referring to several things. He might be simply saying that they eat too much, indulging their gluttony. It is just possible that the word for belly is a reference to human reproductive organs, indicating that they were sexually immoral. However, perhaps the most straightforward is to understand this in terms of all that Paul has said so far in the chapter about trusting in the Law for righteousness. In Colossians 2 we see that the Law-worshippers trusted in the dietary laws of Moses: they made a 'god' of what they did and didn't eat.

We see the same issue facing Peter in Acts 10:9-29. Jesus forced Peter to realise that the dietary laws were only temporary signs of the division between Jew and Gentile. After Jesus fulfilled the Law, after Israel had gone out to the whole world, the dietary signs were no longer binding. The circumcision fanatics would clearly have continued to enforce the dietary laws on the Gentiles, insisting that they could not be righteous before the LORD God unless they kept the whole Law.

In verses 20-21 Paul returns to the key issue that faces the Philippians, as we noted in connection with 1:27. The city of Philippi took such pride in Roman citizenship. The "circumcisers" and the Philippian pagans had at least one thing in common: they were utterly earthly-minded. The Philippian Christians had to show another way.

We are citizens of Jesus' Heavenly Kingdom.

Whatever nationality we are in this passing age, our true patriotism is owed to King Jesus.

We are first citizens of Heaven and only in a very much lesser sense citizens of any earthly kingdom.

This has many consequences:

1. Our hopes and investments are set in the Kingdom of Jesus. We are trying to invest our time and possessions and talent in the advancement of the gospel, storing up the treasure of spiritual fruit for eternity.

2. In today's world, issues of nationalism are growing. Whether in terms of Western democracy or in terms of Islam or in terms of cultural pride, patriotism has become a very treasured idea. Churches in each country have different details to face, but we all face the same big principle. We can never give our fundamental allegiance to our earthly kingdom. It is vital that the Christian church always stands above and beyond the agendas of this passing age. Even if our nation is at war with another, yet our fellowship with the Christians in the opposing country will always come first.

The enemies of the Cross of Christ are set on the *earthly*, but the citizen of Jesus is set on the *heavenly*.

The Philippian citizens seemed to have their eye on the judicial authority of Rome, but the Christian lives in the knowledge that the Great Judge Jesus is the only One whose judgement really matters.

Paul explains the key feature of our heavenly citizenship. We are *eagerly* waiting for Jesus to return (verse 20). He has power over everything and when He returns He will give resurrection, immortal, physical bodies to every believer from all of history. *That* is what fills the future hope of every true believer.

Whatever things lie in our earthly future, they are all set aside as little and momentary (Romans 8:18-25) when seen in the glorious light of Jesus' return.

If we have set our hearts and minds on that fabulous future, then it will be obvious in the way that we live our lives every single day.

Jesus "will transform our lowly bodies so that they will be like His glorious body". What a reassuring future that is! Every one of us sees and experiences, sooner or later, the curse of death and decay that lies on us. Most of us will have experienced a degree of vitality and strength in our youth... but how brief that time is! Sooner or later these lowly bodies return to the dust that we came from. Yet... and we need to remind ourselves of it every single day... Jesus has absolutely guaranteed to us that when He returns we will receive a body *just like His glorious body*.[42]

SUGGESTED QUESTIONS FOR 'THE POWER OF HIS RESURRECTION AND THE FELLOWSHIP OF SHARING IN HIS SUFFERINGS'. 3:1-21

1. In light of the sufferings that the Philippian church was going through according to 1:29-30, why is 3:1 surprising? (Compare Luke 6:22-23.) How is it possible?

2. Why is Paul's language so strong in verse 2?

3. Read Acts 15:1. What does this tell us about the nature and seriousness of the sort of false teaching that was being promoted at this time?

4. What is true circumcision about? Compare Deuteronomy 10:16, Jeremiah 9:25-26, Colossians 2:11.

5. What does the expression "confidence in the flesh" mean? Verse 3.

6. How does Paul view all of his qualifications and credentials in the light of his relationship with Jesus (verse 7)?

    What things might we take pride in, instead of trusting Jesus?

7. How does Paul describe true righteousness in verse 9?

8. What is the one thing that Paul seeks above everything else? Verse 10.

    Is this true for you? How can we obtain this?

9. What aspects of Jesus does Paul seek to know and share according to verses 10-11?

10. How does Paul view himself according to verse 12?

    How does this make him live according to verses 12-14?

    How can we adopt the same attitude?

11. Compare Paul's description of the life and future of the false teachers with his description of the life and future of the Christian in verses 19-21? What do you notice?

12. What can we learn about our resurrection from verses 20-21?

6. Rejoice in the Lord, always. 4:1-23

"Rejoice in trials"

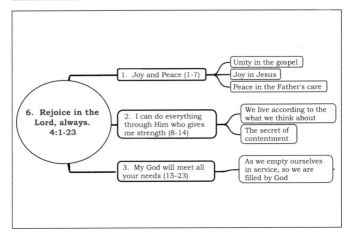

1. JOY AND PEACE (1-7)

Paul reaches the conclusion to what he began in 1:27. Let's remind ourselves of it once more:

> **1:27-28a** "Whatever happens, live as a citizen worthy of the gospel of Christ. Then, whether I come and see you or only hear about you in my absence, I will know that you *stand firm* in one spirit, contending as one man for the faith of the gospel without being frightened in any way by those who oppose you."

Paul has spent the letter showing the Philippian church how to *stand firm in the Lord,* united in the work of the gospel. He showed them how they can be united together – against self-interest in chapter 2 and against false teaching in chapter 3.

So, Paul reaches his conclusion with such affection words of love and encouragement.

> "The description of the readers as (my crown) reminds us of 2:16, where he called them his 'boast on the day of Christ'... It is one of the most intimate touches in Paul, which we understand when it begins to

dawn on us how he hopes to stand *then* – then, in the great *Then* of the fulfilment – adorned by those whom... he has brought... to the Lord, presenting to the Lord His elect, to the Head, His Body, the Church.[43] "

Paul is doing just what he said in 3:20 – he is waiting eagerly for *that Day* when he would be standing with the Philippian Christians in the presence of Jesus entering into the everlasting glory of the New Creation.

However, there is still some business to do. The harsh warnings of chapter 3 are behind us now, and Paul has much more gentle words to say to these two women in verses 2-3.

First we need to clear up a translation problem. If you read verse 2 in the NIV translation you are left wondering who "loyal yoke-fellow" is. It is almost as if the whole letter has been written to some "loyal yoke-fellow" whose identity is kept hidden from us. [44] However, the NIV translators have translated what is probably the name of a man! Just as Paul means "small" and Peter means "rock", so Sudzuge means "loyal yokefellow" or "true comrade". The verse should read, "Yes, and I ask you, Sudzuge, help these women..." [45]

Paul *pleads* with Euodia and Syntyche because it is so tragic that they disagree with each other. Paul doesn't tell us what they disagreed about, so we can imagine all the disagreements that we have ever had with other Christians. Whatever the grievance, the answer is the same. They have both "contended" at Paul's side "in the cause of the gospel". When they were doing that they enjoyed great unity, but now they have become divided. It is just as we learnt earlier in the letter. We find amazing unity as we stand together in the cause of the gospel. We find that all the differences that the flesh might use to divide are put into the liberating perspective of eternity when we stand together holding out the word of truth to the world.

A minister I have worked with, Rev Paul Williams, finds this verse so exciting because it is so true to our experience. When he has led a team of Christians for a mission week, he describes how they usually will say something like "I have never enjoyed Christian fellowship so much as this!" Of course that is true!

---

[43] Barth, 117

[44] People who have translated the verse in the way that the NIV has done have suggested that it might be Epaphroditus, Silas or Luke.

[45] It is interesting to note that Syntyche means "common fate" and Euodia means "fragrant" ("good smell"). "I plead with Good Smell and Common Fate to agree with each other... helped by True Comrade."

In our new birth we have been given the *gospel* nature of Jesus and we truly "find ourselves" as we stand together, side by side, in the cause of the gospel.

Clement is mentioned here in verse 3 as another of Paul's fellow-workers. He too enjoyed fellowship with Paul in the cause of the gospel. This is probably the Clement (of Rome) who went on to become one of the great church leaders in the apostolic church. He lived from about 30AD to 100AD, and met Paul at Philippi. He wrote two letters to the Corinthian church, which you might like to read.[46] This letter of Paul clearly made a strong impression on Clement because he writes at such length with such passion about the need for *church unity*.

When I was young I sometimes worried about my assurance of salvation. In my doubting I often used to think of Clement with great envy because, I thought, he was a man who could have absolutely no assurance problems. The Bible, the very Word of God, told him personally that his name was in the Book of Life![47] The problem with my thinking was that I was focussing on myself and not on Jesus. If we get assurance from anything other than our trusting in Jesus, then it is not a real assurance.

Christ died for our sins and rose again and stands at the right hand of the Father. *That* is the only reason that I have assurance of salvation.

As you read this study guide you too might worry if you are really saved, or you might talk to another Christian who is like that. The only way out of *that* is to look away from yourself and your own feelings and experiences and look only to Jesus Himself. Give yourself to studying His Cross and Resurrection. Read His teaching, understand His ascension. Fix your mind and heart on Him, knowing that in Him we have the eternal love and acceptance of the Living God. That old piece of advice is more true here than anywhere: for every look at self, take 10 looks at Jesus.

Notice that we must stand firm *in the Lord* (verse 1); that Euodia and Syntyche must agree *in the Lord* (verse 2); that we rejoice *in the Lord* (verse 4).

Everything in the Christian life is in *Jesus*.

We can stand firm only as we look to Him and are strengthened by Him. We can find agreement with each other only as we share the mind of Jesus,

---

46 www.ccel.org

47 This "book of life" is mentioned in Exodus 32:32; Psalm 69:28 and in Luke 10:20. However, it is most frequently mentioned in Revelation: 3:5; 18:8; 20:12.

holding out the truth about Him to the world. We rejoice with the unspeakable joy that *He* gives. If we try to stand firm with our own schemes; if we think we can maintain true faith and teaching with mere documents or human zeal then we are doomed to bitter disappointment. We stand firm only when we look to Jesus to hold us.

If we try to establish church unity through politics or by finding a lowest common denominator then we are fools. We know unity, strength and joy only as we rally around Jesus, finding in Him our common mind as He opens our minds to the Scriptures and sends us out with His life-giving gospel.

Paul has commanded joy before in the letter, and now he does it twice in one verse (verse 4): "*Rejoice* in the Lord always. I will say it again: *Rejoice!*"

Is Paul saying, "Chin up! It might not happen – you must keep smiling!" or some other irritating pleasantry? Is he commanding that we simply look happy and positive? NO! Remember what he said at the end of chapter 3.

> **Philippians 3:20-21** "Our citizenship is in heaven. And we eagerly await a Saviour from there, the Lord Jesus Christ, who, by the power that enables him to bring everything under his control, will transform our lowly bodies so that they will be like his glorious body."

Paul's argument is much more substantial than "keep smiling!" He lifts the Philippians' vision to the future, where our real glory lies. He wants us all to have a true perspective on life and history, so that we neither despair about the bad times nor become over-confident about the good times. We eagerly await a Saviour from heaven, Jesus, who will give us physical bodies just like His glorious physical body.

So, when he tells us to *always* rejoice in the LORD, he is reminding us of the real basis of our hope and confidence, the real rock solid centre of our joy. All the ups and downs of life can be seen for what they are – "momentary and light", as he says in 2 Corinthians 4:16-18.

> **2 Corinthians 4:16-18** "We do not lose heart. Though outwardly we are wasting away, yet inwardly we are being renewed day by day. For our light and momentary troubles are achieving for us an eternal glory that far outweighs them all. So we fix our eyes not on what is seen, but on what is unseen. For what is seen is temporary, but what is unseen is eternal."

Yes, even our earthly successes as well as our sufferings are just momentary and light compared to the glorious hope we have in the return of Jesus. The LORD is near (verse 5).

Nothing that can happen to us now, either good or bad, can compare to what is to come.

Very early in the morning on December 25th each year, our children wake up with enormous excitement. The joy actually begins much earlier in December as they begin to anticipate something nice on Christmas morning. It is amazing how that joy of anticipation is able to lift their mood more and more as the day draws near. I used to get a similar feeling when I was at school, towards of the end of the summer term, as I anticipated going on a family holiday.

The joy that Paul focuses on here is a joy that does not depend on our current situation, but on the fact that "the Lord is near". The glory of Jesus' return is almost upon us... so we are not crushed by the things that we may face right now. All things can be endured, not with stoical grit, but with great joy in Jesus, if we set our hearts and minds on our glorious future. If Jesus is everything to us, then knowing that we will meet Him soon, fills us with unspeakable joy.

So, Philippians 4:4, we must learn to *rejoice* in the LORD *at all times*. It's such a good piece of advice that Paul repeats it. Only in this way can we fulfill the further advice of verse 6 – "Do not be anxious about anything, but in everything, by prayer and petition, with thanksgiving, present your requests to God."

I love this verse. It was one of the first verses I ever learned. It got slightly spoiled for me for a while when I heard a preacher say it was a stern divine command, and if I disobeyed it the LORD would punish me. Therefore I spent about 18 months worried that I was worrying too much! Obviously, this verse isn't like that. It is the loving reassurance of our Abba Father who tells us to leave all the worrying to Him. He is our All-powerful spiritual Father and He's watching out for us – so there's simply no point in us getting worked up about things.

The key to the whole verse is that we present all our requests to our Father with *thanksgiving*. No matter what our circumstance we are always full of deep gratitude to our Father. Such constant thanksgiving comes when we are always remembering the immeasureable grace and favour that is ours in Jesus. There was an old lady at All Souls who suffered terrible ill health for years and yet she would always say, with complete sincerity, "I am a spiritual millionaire!" She was always full of thanksgiving.

This verse reminds us so much of the teaching of Jesus in the Sermon on the Mount. After teaching us how to pray, He tells us:

Matthew 6:25-34 "*Do not worry* about your life, what you will eat or drink; or about your body, what you will wear. Is not life more important than food, and the body more important than clothes? Look at the birds of the air; they do not sow or reap or store away in barns, and yet your heavenly Father feeds them. Are you not much more valuable than they? Who of you by worrying can add a single hour to his life? And *why do you worry* about clothes?... So *do not worry*, saying, `What shall we eat?' or `What shall we drink?' or `What shall we wear?' For the pagans run after all these things, and your heavenly Father knows that you need them. But seek first his kingdom and his righteousness, and all these things will be given to you as well. Therefore *do not worry* about tomorrow, for tomorrow will worry about itself. Each day has enough trouble of its own."

See how often Jesus tells us not to worry about all the day to day things that we worry so much about. After teaching us how to pray He tells us not to worry. The two things go together as Paul teaches us here in Philippians.

Our daily habit should be to talk to our Father about everything that's on our mind, asking Him for all the things that bother us. In this way, verse 7, we will come to know "the peace of God, which transcends all understanding", which will guard our hearts and our minds in Christ Jesus.

This peace is not a peace which can only exist in the cloistered serenity of a darkened prayer room while meditating on a candle or that depends on having gentle music on our CD player. It is the peace of GOD that stays with us even in the worst and most painful earthly disasters. In the turmoil of suffering we may know this peace. We may know that we are safe in our

Father's keeping; utterly secure in Jesus whatever may happen to us.

It is the wonderful peace that is ours when we know the truth of Romans 8:35-39.

> "Who shall separate us from the love of Christ? Shall trouble or hardship or persecution or famine or nakedness or danger or sword? As it is written: 'For your sake we face death all day long; we are considered as sheep to be slaughtered.' No, in all these things we are more than conquerors through him who loved us. For I am convinced that neither death nor life, neither angels nor demons, neither the present nor the future, nor any powers, neither height nor depth, nor anything else in all creation, will be able to separate us from the love of God that is in Christ Jesus our Lord."

2. I CAN DO EVERYTHING THROUGH HIM WHO GIVES ME STRENGTH (8-14)

Paul has thoroughly laid the foundations for what he tells us in verses 8-13. Since chapter 3 he has been showing us that we need to run empty-handed towards the future where Jesus has everything to give to us. This prevents us being crushed by the pains and pleasures of this passing age and fills us with amazing joy. Each day we depend entirely on our Father and trust Him to care for us.

But, is this realistic? How can we keep our minds fixed on these glorious gospel truths? How can we keep our hearts fixed on Jesus? So many Christians complain that the "world" captures their heart and mind so that Jesus seems far away. Paul is very aware of this very common problem, so he tells us exactly what to do.

In verse 8 & 9, Paul passes on some excellent Christian advice to help us keep this Christian mind at all times. I constantly find that I lose my Christian perspective because of what I feed my mind with. Sometimes I start to yearn for earthly success or I start to dislike the cost of following the way of Jesus. Why? Because I have allowed myself to think about things that I shouldn't have.

Philippians 4:8-9 is the apostle Paul's guide to mental health.

Mental discipline is an overlooked area of Christian discipleship. *What we think about will set the level of our Christian living*. What feeds our imagination will surface in all kinds of ways in day-to-day life – especially in the way we handle success and failure. We cannot ultimately hide what we think about.

We cannot secretly fantasise about winning the lottery without consequences. We cannot secretly think about earthly treasure and pleasure without becoming caught by those thoughts. We cannot feed our lusts and then simply walk away from them. We cannot indulge our greedy thoughts and then put them safely back in our mental cupboard. No, if we set our thoughts on worldly things then we will quickly lose our Christian heart and mind. If we mentally invest in what the flesh craves, then we will find that the things of the Spirit fade away from our daily agenda. If we think like the world we will be unable to deal with earthly success and failure properly.

If our minds are not serving Jesus, we will lose what it is to hope and joy in the LORD. If we think about fleshly treasures and pleasures we will want them more than our Saviour from heaven (3:20-21).

Be very, very careful what you watch on TV, what you read, what you discuss or joke about, what you do with your leisure time. What kind of games do you play? What kind of films do you watch?

Paul's remedy is for us to guard our minds very carefully. We must constantly monitor what we think about. He gives us a list of qualities to look for in our mental diet. If our mental diet is full of these things then we will remain in the daily habits of verses 4-7.

But verse 8 seems a bit abstract. What does such a mental approach look like in practice? Paul offers himself as a model of all that he has been saying (verse 9). We have so much information about the life of Paul in the Book of Acts and so much autobiographical material in all his letters that we can know this apostle very well. We know what troubles he faced, and we know he endured these troubles. We know what things absorbed his mind day by day. We know that whether he was working as a leather-worker, travelling around the Mediterranean or planting churches his mind was full of the Scriptures, full of the gospel, full of concern for other Christians, full of prayer, constantly looking for evangelistic opportunities.

As we study the life and writings of Paul we should be studying his mental diet: what was his mind occupied with?

But, it is not only the way that Paul thinks that is in view in verse 9. The whole of Paul's life is to be studied. We are to live as Paul lived, as he told us in 3:17.

In verse 10 and 14 Paul is happy that these fellow workers in the gospel share in his sufferings with him.

Not only is that a great encouragement and comfort for Paul, but it shows that they have become mature Christians. They are not locked into their own problems, always praying for blessings on themselves, but they have become aware of other members of the Christian Body and view the ups and downs of other Christians as their own ups and downs. Just that one fact helps us to keep a proper balance in the face of earthly success and failure.

We are always sharing in the life of our brothers and sisters, some of whom are up when we are down, and some are down when we are up. Because we share our life together we are all strengthened. When you are rich, you can help me in my poverty – and then when things turn around, I will do the same for you (see 2 Corinthians 8:14). This must be especially true when our troubles come in the cause of the gospel, as was the case with Paul. When we are persecuted for the gospel, nothing is so precious to us as Christian fellowship.

But, it is verses 11-13 that are the centre-piece of Paul's testimony in Philippians –

> "I have learned to be content whatever the circumstances. I know what it is to be in need, and I know what it is to have plenty. I have learned the secret of being content in any and every situation, whether well fed or hungry, whether living in plenty or in want. I can do everything through him who gives me strength."

Paul had learned to be content whatever the circumstances, whether rich or poor, whether in sickness or in health. He had discovered the secret of this contentment. Well, what is it?

"I can do everything through Jesus who gives me strength."

Nothing is too much for us, nothing can overwhelm us, because we lean on Jesus for our strength. We know, (don't we?), that there are all kinds of human suffering that we could never face in our own strength. We know (don't we?) that there are all kinds of earthly successes and treasures that would ruin our Christian discipleship, in our own strength. Therefore, we keep tightly hold of the hope that is before us, the faith of Jesus Christ.

Our flesh wants to be *self*-serving and *earthly*-minded. The way to true contentment is to lose our life, to give ourselves away in the service of Jesus. We might naturally think that we will be content only when we satisfy our desires and perceived needs. The secret of contentment is that when we try to grasp onto life in *that* way, it always slips away from us. When we forget ourselves and follow Jesus in love and service, then we actually gain life and fulfilment and joy and contentment.

> **Matthew 16:24-25** "Jesus said to His disciples, "If anyone would come after me, he must deny himself and take up his cross and

follow me. For whoever wants to save his life will lose it, but whoever loses his life for me will find it."

Paul had to *learn* to do this. It didn't come naturally to him anymore than to us. Our sinful hearts and minds will always want to grumble in the hard times and glory in the good times. But, with Paul we must learn day by day to be content as we trust in the strength of Jesus alone, fully aware of our own utter weakness. It is the mark of Christian discipleship. It is something we need to daily practice.

Spurgeon, in his *Morning and Evening* daily devotions has a very helpful meditation on this passage:

"These words show us that contentment is not a natural propensity of man. 'Ill weeds grow apace.' Covetousness, discontent, and murmuring are as natural to man as thorns are to the soil. We need not sow thistles and brambles; they come up naturally enough, because they are indigenous to earth: and so, we need not teach men to complain; they complain fast enough without any education. But the precious things of the earth must be cultivated... *Paul says, 'I have learned ... to be content;' as much as to say, he did not know how at one time.* It cost him some pains to attain to the mystery of that great truth. No doubt he sometimes thought he had learned, and then broke down. And when at last he had attained unto it, and could say, 'I have learned in whatsoever state I am, therewith to be content,' he was an old, grey-headed man, upon the borders of the grave-a poor prisoner shut up in Nero's dungeon at Rome. We might well be willing to endure Paul's infirmities, and share the cold dungeon with him, if we too might by any means attain unto his good degree... Brother, hush that murmur, natural though it be, and continue a diligent pupil in the College of Content."

If we don't daily feed our minds with the things of Christ, in the Bible and prayer, then the secret of contentment will forever elude us. If we daily feed our minds with the health and wealth desires of the flesh, with the fantasies of our evil desires then we will know only the secret of discontentment.

3. MY GOD WILL MEET ALL YOUR NEEDS (15-23)

As the letter comes to its conclusion, Paul recalls the great generosity that the Philippians had shown towards him. In the month that he had been at Thessalonica (verse 16) they had sent him at least two packages of aid. Paul had mentioned this kindness at the beginning of the letter, but now he more formally thanks them.

The other churches had not *shared* with Paul in all his struggles for the gospel (verse 15). The Philippians had seen Paul's gospel work as their own and had funded it properly. Paul doesn't mention this as a subtle way of asking for another cheque (verse 17). He simply wants to note that in doing this they have produced fruit which they will be able to show on the Day of Christ.

Examine your own finances and the finances of your local church family. Do they reflect your commitment to the cause of the gospel? How is your money helping the work of evangelism? Rev Paul Williams once said a very striking thing to me – "Only Christians will fund evangelism." If we do not pay for the work of evangelists and missionaries, if we do not give money to gospel work in our own area and across the world, then who will? The world will never do it. The governments won't. The unbelieving world will give money to all the many good causes in our world, but only Christians care about the gospel of Jesus Christ.

There are thrilling opportunites to fund evangelists in the world today. Let me give you one wonderful example. Gospel for Asia is an evangelistic organisation determined to send out *Asian* evangelists across Asia. For between £50 and £100 a month you can fund an evangelist. Go to www.gfa.org/gfa/sponsor for more information.

In verse 18 Paul thanks them again. They sent money and Epaphroditus so that Paul got all that he needed. Again, Paul helps them to see that their generosity is not simply a personal matter between him and the Philippians. In putting the cause of the gospel on their agenda in such a practical way, they have brought great pleasure to God the Father. He describes their support for the gospel as "a fragrant offering". Back in 2:17 Paul had portrayed the gospel work of the Philippians as a sacrifice, with his own work as the concluding drink offering. Here he draws attention to the effect this has on our Heavenly Father. When He sees how we share the gospel passion of Jesus He is pleased. When the Father "smells" the evangelistic commitment of a local church family He is pleased.

The Philippians gave to Paul… but Paul is showing how all that they have done is to the Father. He cannot repay the Philippians, but because their generosity is really an offering to the Father, Paul assures them that the Father will care for them with the infinite riches that are in Jesus. They will receive far more in Jesus than they ever lose in giving for the gospel. [48]

The great 18th century Bible scholar Matthew Henry comments on this:

> "He does as it were draw a bill upon the exchequer in heaven, and leaves it to God to make them amends for the kindness they had shown him. 'He shall do it, not only as your God, but as my God, who takes what is done to me as done to Himself. You supplied my needs, according to your poverty; and He shall supply yours, according to His riches.' But still it is by Christ Jesus; through Him we have grace to do that which is good, and through Him we must expect the reward of it. *Not of debt, but of grace*; for the more we do for God the more we are indebted to Him, because we receive the more from Him."

Thus, the letter concludes with all the glory going to God the Father. We have *nothing*… yet He has freely given us *everything* in Jesus. Even our willing and acting (2:13) is a free gift from Him. If we give our money or time to others, we find ourselves with more treasure than we ever give away.

The very end of the letter gives us an exciting glimpse of the gospel in Caesar's own household. The Roman empire may have seemed like an empire that could never pass away, and yet right there the everlasting Kingdom of Jesus was advancing in the basement of Caesar's palace. Members of Caesar's staff were following the true Ruler of the world even while they worked at the centre of the empire. Their citizenship was in heaven, while living in the place that pagans in the city of Philippi most revered. Paul wanted the Philippians to know that even Caesar had no defence against the power of the Living God in the gospel of Jesus Christ.

---

[48] We must beware of those false teachers that sometimes appear on TV who claim that verses like this refer to earthly money. The Bible never promises that if we give money to some kind of 'ministry' we will get lots of money back. That kind of teaching is worldly, fleshly greed trying to deceive people. When these wolves in sheepskin coats say that we must give up our money, even if we have none, "to plant a seed of faith" in order to "reap a great financial blessing", we must run away from them as quickly as we can.

SUGGESTED QUESTIONS FOR 'REJOICE IN THE LORD, ALWAYS'. 4:1-23

1. How is Paul's plea to Euodia and Syntyche connected to the theme of this letter? (Compare 1:27, 2:2.)

2. What three actions are mentioned as "in the Lord" in verses 1-4?

   What does the expression "in the Lord" mean?

3. How is it possible to "rejoice in the Lord always"?

   Read 3:20-21 again. (Compare 2 Corinthians 4:16-18.)

4. Describe the life of someone who lives according to the teaching of verses 4-6? Does this describe your life?

5. What can we do when we sense we are becoming worried or anxious about things? Verse 7.

6. Why is Paul so concerned about what the Philippian Christians think about in verse 8? What effect does our thinking have on our actions? (Compare Colossians 3:2.)

7. In what ways is verse 9 connected to verse 8? (Compare 3:17.)

8. Why does Paul describe being content in any and every situation as a "secret"? How can we learn this secret?

9. How is Paul able to do all things and endure all things according to verse 13?

10. As Paul was only in Thessalonica for less than a month (Acts 17:2) what does verse 16 tell us about the way the Philippian church gave money for gospel work?

    How much money do you give to the work of spreading the good news of Jesus Christ?

11. Who else is pleased by the Philippians' generosity according to verse 18? What does this tell us about our giving?

12. How can we be encouraged by the fact that there were "saints" and citizens of heaven even among "those who belong to Caesar's household"?

13. How can the example of Paul and the example of the Philippian church serve to challenge and strengthen us in the work of sharing the great news about Jesus Christ?

Bible Study hints and helps

Not all the questions have hints and helps. Some of the Bible study questions are simply designed to make us reflect on our own walk with Jesus.

STUDY 1

1. Paul writes to ALL the saints. A theme of the letter is unity, so he begins with everyone in mind.

2. The saints are not specially advanced Christians. In the Bible a person is a saint the very moment they trust in Jesus. We are 'holy' in Jesus, no matter how we might feel or how others may view us.

3. The Philippian saints not only preach and live the gospel in their own situation, but they are supporting gospel work in other places. They have given money to support Paul's gospel work.

4. He prays with joy because he knows for sure that the gospel of Jesus can deliver the Philippians to 'completion' on the day of Jesus. It is almost as if he can see the end already.

5. Paul loves the Philippians as fellow members of God's family, because they too enjoy God's grace. Every Christian we meet is an eternal family member. The affection he has for them flows from the Lord Jesus Himself. It is not just our own feeble love in our hearts, but the love of Jesus that is given to us.

6. The love of the saints needs to grow, but they also need to learn more about how to love each other. Their love must be more than good intentions. It must be practical and effective and enduring. This kind of love shows us how we should act so that we can live fruitful lives.

7. Too often our 'fellowship' is nothing more than sharing a hot drink after a church service. Our love needs to be deeper and more thoughtful so that members of the Christian family are not overlooked.

STUDY 2

1. Paul's imprisonment is actually a way for the gospel to go forward. His focus is not on his own problems, but on the gospel of Jesus.

2. Some have seen how faithful Paul is even in prison and so were encouraged to witness to Jesus. Others took advantage of Paul's situation to make trouble for him. It seems odd that both groups were preaching Jesus.

3. Paul has no concern about his own personal status or prestige. As long as Jesus is on the public agenda, as long as the gospel is being communicated, Paul is joyful.

4. Paul is not sure about being released from prison, but he is confident that the Spirit will keep him fruitful and faithful. Paul wants to be delivered from a life that does not bring glory to Jesus.

5. Present day sufferings may make us quiet about Jesus.

7. Paul is prepared to put his own desires aside for the sake of other people. He shows what it is to think of others above yourself.

8. The Philippians thought very highly of being Roman citizens. If the Philippian saints lived as if only heaven mattered to them, it would be very counter-cultural.

10. Witnessing to Jesus always brings a collision with the world around us.

11. Just as Paul did not fear death because of his love for Jesus, so the same witness can be shown in the way we witness fearlessly.

12. Their sufferings are not a punishment but a privilege. When we are treated the same way that the world treated Jesus, we know the honour and respect of God.

STUDY 3

1. There are so many encouragements given to us in Jesus that we can bear all kinds of hardships.

2. Christian unity is so often Paul's great passion. We can so easily argue and divide over trivial and personal problems; yet following the example of Jesus will show us another way.

3. We can only be united together when we put other people ahead of our own personal concerns. We naturally put our own interests first. We tend to assume that we will only be happy if we chase after our own desires and ideas.

5. If we all look out for each other's interests in the church family, then there will be many people looking after my interests. Would this make a major difference to your own church situation? Are there neglected people?

6. Verses 5-11 show us the ultimate example of all that Paul has been talking about in verses 1-4.

7. Jesus is both the Living God and the lowly, human servant of us. It turns human values upside down. In human society, servants do not have the glory and honour and status of the celebrities. Jesus seemed to be so humble and lowly... yet He was also the Creator and Lord of the Universe.

8. Jesus had so much personal wealth and glory and comfort, yet He was ready to set it all aside to help us. Jesus is the ultimate example of caring for others at extreme personal cost. Whenever we hold onto our money, privileges, comfort or time, we chose a different way than the way of Jesus.

9. Each day we have to give up our life for Jesus and for others. It cannot be done just once when we first became a Christian. It is our daily pattern.

10. Jesus was given the honour and praise of the Most High God after His time of humble service. We too will know the honour of our Heavenly Father when we serve as Jesus served.

STUDY 4

1. Studying the example of Jesus is supposed to lead to a change in our own living. What practical things can you do to follow this way of Jesus?

2. We are in "fear and trembling" when we consider how utterly weak we are. When we think of how we must live to follow Jesus we are reduced to trembling wrecks! Yet, this drives us to trust in Jesus. Without His strength and care we could do nothing.

3. If we are denying our selfish desires and giving up our comforts, privileges and money for others, then our sinful nature will always want to complain. The life of Jesus is war against the old life of sinful self. There will always be protests from that old nature until Jesus comes again.

4. Are there any parts of Jesus' teaching that particularly clash with our own culture. In the modern West a young Christian can seem very different if they refuse to date until they find the one they will marry; if they refuse to date a non-Christian; and if they refuse all sexual intimacy until marriage. Older Christians might make a similar impact if they do not work towards a dream retirement, with a big house and lots of money.

5. We have only one life. When we die, our opportunities for service and fruitfulness are over. We waste our lives if we live to do the kind of things that we will be able to do in the New Creation. Think about the ways that we can serve Jesus now that will be impossible in that glorious future.

6. For Paul it is always, Jesus first, others second and himself last of all.

7. Timothy put the interests of others ahead of his own.

8. Epaphroditus is Paul's "brother, fellow-worker and fellow-soldier" and he is the "messenger" of the Philippians. Think of the relationships and service that each of these words imply.

STUDY 5

1. Paul is suffering along with the Philippians, yet they are *commanded* to rejoice even then. Romans 14:17 "the kingdom of God is not a matter of eating and drinking, but of righteousness, peace and joy in the Holy Spirit."

2. Paul cares so much for the Philippians. Anyone who tries to harm them makes Paul very upset and protective. He sees the terrible danger in what is happening to the Philippian church.

3. This is not a mere theory or abstract debate. This is about salvation. This issue is so serious that anyone who gets it wrong will go to Hell.

4. Circumcision was only a sign or shadow of a wonderful spiritual reality. The circumcision that God really wants is the new birth of the Spirit. Our Father looks for those whose hearts are cut and renewed.

5. To trust in the 'flesh' is to trust in the powers and goodness of our old, natural human nature… as if we could be good enough to impress our Holy Father.

6. All the best things Paul had achieved were dismissed as manure or dung because they are so much less than his relationship with Jesus. We might take pride in our family background, our friends, our career, even our schooling.

7. True righteousness comes *from* God and is not created by our own human effort. It is received when we *trust* in Jesus rather than trying to impress God.

8. To know Jesus is the very highest thing in life or death, for the apostle Paul. We love Jesus more, the more we get to know about Him, the more we obey His teaching, the more we trust Him.

9. The Cross and the Resurrection are the foundation stones of our experience of Jesus each day. In our sufferings we fellowship with Jesus as we experience, even then, our resurrection life.

10. Paul has no confidence in his own achievements or abilities. He sees himself as needing a lot of work from Jesus. He knows that as long as he keeps trusting Jesus and going forward in obedience to Jesus, then Jesus will hold onto him and bring him to the resurrection future.

11. Paul was trying to be like Jesus, to reach towards Jesus. Therefore all Christians love to follow His example.

12. Our future resurrection is not a ghostly existence, but a wonderful and glorious transformation of our physical bodies. We will always have these physical bodies.

STUDY 6

1. Getting on with each other and serving each other is the great theme of the book. If these two could sort out their feud, then it would show that the way of Jesus works, right there and then in the Philippian church.

2. Stand firm, agree with each other and rejoice always: all three must be in the Lord. To be "in the Lord" means to be relying only on His strength and power.

3. We receive joy from the Spirit and we need to fix our hearts and minds on the glorious New Creation future guaranteed to us.

4. Our heavenly Father can give us a peace that seems entirely miraculous. Sometimes we can experience this peace when outside everything is severe conflict and opposition.

5. Whatever we feed our minds and hearts with will become part of our daily behaviour, attitudes and habits.

6. Paul has shown them how to do what he says. He has, also, taught them many things that are full of the good things that he lists.

7. The 'secret' of contentment is invisible from the outside. People would always assume that giving away your time, money, comfort or service for 'nothing' will make us unhappy. However, when we trust the way of Jesus and do what he says even though it goes against our natural instincts… then we find 'the secret of contentment'.

8. Again, in 'fear and trembling' Paul knows his own weakness. Yet he also knows the infinite power of Jesus. Paul knows that he can do anything if he is relying only on Jesus.

9. The Philippians frequently sent money to Paul. They were eager to go without things so that others could hear the gospel.

10. Our Father is pleased by our giving. When we give to others, it is the Father who rewards us with His friendship and honour.

11. No empire, no fortress is strong enough to withstand Jesus and His gospel! Caesar thought he had the gospel locked away in his basement, yet it was busy transforming the jailers. Our gospel message is dynamite.

12. Paul has shown us what it really means to follow Jesus. Serving others is not optional. Sharing the gospel with our non-Christian friends is not optional. Yet, in the service and self-denial there is glory and fellowship with Jesus.